DIVINE SAYINGS

Also available from Anqa Publishing

Contemplation of the Holy Mysteries: mashāhid al-asrār,
by Ibn ʿArabī
Translated by Cecilia Twinch and Pablo Beneito

The Universal Tree and the Four Birds: al-ittiḥād al-kawnī,
by Ibn ʿArabī
Translated by Angela Jaffray

A Prayer for Spiritual Elevation and Protection: al-dawr al-aʿlā,
by Ibn ʿArabī
Study, translation, transliteration and Arabi text
by Suha Taji-Farouki

The Unlimited Mercifier: the Spiritual Life and Thought of Ibn ʿArabī
Stephen Hirtenstein

Ibn ʿArabi and Modern Thought:
The History of Taking Metaphysics Seriously
Peter Coates

The Nightingale in the Garden of Love: the Poems of Üftade
by Paul Ballanfat
Translated from French by Angela Culme-Seymour

Beshara and Ibn ʿArabi:
A Movement of Sufi Spirituality in the Modern World
Suha Taji-Farouki

Muḥyīddīn Ibn ʿArabī

DIVINE SAYINGS

101 Ḥadīth Qudsī

Mishkāt al-anwār

TRANSLATED BY
STEPHEN HIRTENSTEIN AND MARTIN NOTCUTT

ANQA PUBLISHING • OXFORD

Published by Anqa Publishing
PO Box 1178
Oxford OX2 8YS, UK
www.ibn-arabi.com

First published 2004
First paperback edition, 2008

A CIP catalogue record for this book is available from the British Library

ISBN 978 1 905937 03 5

Jacket design by Gerard Lennox

Back cover: Ibn ʿArabī's signature
(courtesy of the Beshara School, Scotland)

Printed and bound in the USA

Contents

THE 101 HADITH QUDSI

PART ONE

PART TWO

PART THREE

Acknowledgements

Little did we realise, when we first began the translation of this book in 1996, just how much work would be involved. We wish to express our deepest gratitude to the following, without whose help and expertise this book would not have seen the light of day.

We are greatly indebted to Daniel Hirtenstein and Sara Sviri for their inestimable help with the translation, and to Rosemary Brass, Sara Hirtenstein, Judy Kearns and Michael Tiernan for their editing, typesetting, proofreading and invaluable suggestions.

We also thank the fellows and members of the Muhyiddin Ibn ʿArabi Society for their support in establishing an archive of Ibn ʿArabī's works, and to the director and staff of the Süleymaniye library in Istanbul for all their help in providing access to these precious manuscripts.

Introduction

The original title of this book by Ibn ʿArabī is "The Niche of Lights concerning some of the communications that have been transmitted from God" (*Mishkāt al-anwār fīmā ruwiya ʿan Allāh min al-akhbār*).

These communications or Divine Sayings are so rich in meaning that it is not possible to characterise them all by a single word or phrase. Recurring themes include our complete dependence on God, and His readiness to forgive and embrace those who truly turn to Him. They are memorable, and in their generosity of spirit bring us close to the absolutely Real. Although they come from the Islamic tradition, and wear the clothes of time and place, they are universal in nature, and can be appreciated by people from any background. The book is a wonderful gift.

The Divine Sayings in the *Mishkāt al-anwār* are called *ḥadīth qudsī* or "sacred sayings", a term which is described more fully in the Appendix, but usually meaning words of God heard by the Prophet Muhammad, and reported outside the Quranic revelation. There are one hundred and one *ḥadīth qudsī* collected together in the *Mishkāt al-anwār*, and most of them are well-known within the Islamic tradition. As the *Mishkāt al-anwār* appears to have been one of the earliest collections of its kind, it may well have played an influential role in making this particular sort of *ḥadīth* literature more popular. Of the several collections of *ḥadīth* made by the celebrated thirteenth-century master, Muḥyīddīn Ibn ʿArabī, this is the only one to have been copied widely.

This is not only a collection by a person well-versed in the science of *ḥadīth* literature, but a selection by a true spiritual master. Indeed, Muḥyīddīn Ibn ʿArabī is known throughout the

Islamic world simply as *al-shaykh al-akbar*, "the greatest master". He dedicated his whole life to exposing, at the deepest level, the primordial Unity underlying all human and natural life, in all its richness and complexity. Author of several hundred works, covering the whole vast range of Islamic mysticism and spiritual thought, he has exerted an unparalleled influence on generations of Muslims. Many of these later students have become beacons of wisdom in their own right. In recent years, as more of his writings have been translated into Western languages, there has been an ever-growing appreciation of his importance as a champion of boundless compassion. This translation of the *Mishkāt al-anwār* is the first in the English language based on a new authoritative edition of the original Arabic.[1]

1. The full Arabic text, based on the earliest manuscripts, can be found in the hardback edition. Previous editions include Muhammad Vâlsan's bilingual version in 1983.

THE 101
HADITH QUDSI

Preface

IN THE NAME OF GOD,
THE ALL-COMPASSIONATE, THE MOST MERCIFUL

And may the blessing of God be upon our master Muhammad, his family and his companions, and peace be upon them all.

The servant who is in utter need of God, Muḥammad ibn ʿAlī ibn Muḥammad ibn al-ʿArabī al-Ṭā'ī al-Ḥātimī al-Andalusī, may God seal him with the best of outcomes, says:

Praise be to God, Lord of the universes, who is the ultimate reward for those who fear Him. There is no power nor might save in God, the High, the Magnificent. May blessings and peace be upon Muhammad, master of the universes, upon his family, the pure ones, and upon his companions, followers and all believers.

According to Ibn ʿAbbās, the Messenger of God, may God give him blessings and peace, said: "Whoever preserves for my community forty *ḥadīth* of the *Sunna*, I shall be his intercessor on the Day of Resurrection." According to Anas ibn Mālik, the Messenger of God, may God give him blessings and peace, also said: "Whoever preserves for my community forty *ḥadīth* of which they stand in need, God shall put him down as learned and knowing."

Having come to know these words of the Prophet, and taking into account that man stands more in need of the other world, which is the place of his return, than this world, I collected these forty *ḥadīth* at Mecca, may God protect it, during the months of the year 599. I took as criterion that they be *ḥadīth* with a chain of transmission going directly back to God, ever exalted is He.

These are followed by forty others, equally going back to God, but without a chain of transmission through the Messenger of God, may God bless him and give him peace, [and these have been selected] from the ones which I have passed on orally and recorded in writing. These I have then completed with twenty-one further *ḥadīth*, making a total of one hundred and one divine *ḥadīth*.

May God profit us and you with knowledge. May He make us one of His people by His grace and His favour, for He is powerful over all things.

PART ONE

FIRST HADITH (1)

According to Abū Dharr, the Prophet, may God give him blessings and peace, said, reporting the words of God, ever praised and exalted is He:

"O My servants, I have forbidden injustice to Myself and I have made it forbidden amongst you. So be not unjust to one another.

"O My servants, all of you go astray except the one whom I guide. Ask guidance of Me, and I shall guide you.

"O My servants, all of you go hungry except the one whom I feed. Ask Me for food, and I shall feed you.

"O My servants, all of you go naked except the one whom I clothe. Ask Me for clothing, and I shall clothe you.

"O My servants, you transgress by day and night, but I forgive all misdeeds. Ask forgiveness of Me, and I shall forgive you.

"O My servants, harming Me is beyond you, so you cannot harm Me; and benefiting Me is beyond you, so you cannot benefit Me.

"O My servants, if all of you – first and last, man and jinn – were like the one among you with the most devout heart, that would add nothing to My kingdom.

"O My servants, if all of you – first and last, man and jinn – were like the one among you with the most ungodly heart, that would take nothing away from My kingdom.

"O My servants, if all of you – first and last, man and jinn – were to stand on the same level and address Me with your requests, and if I were to give each one what he had requested, that would not diminish what is with Me, any more than a needle diminishes the sea when it enters it.[1]

"O My servants, it is solely your deeds that I take account of, and it is by virtue of them that I will repay you. So let him who finds good, praise God, and let him who finds other than that, hold none but himself to blame."

SECOND HADITH (2)

According to Abū Hurayra, the Messenger of God, may God give him blessings and peace, said:

God, ever mighty and majestic is He, says: "Of all the associates, I am the most able to dispense with association. As for him who performs a deed in which there is association with other than Me, I am quit of him, and he belongs to what he has associated [with Me]."[2]

THIRD HADITH (3)

According to Abū Umāma, the Prophet, may God give him blessings and peace, said:

God, ever mighty and majestic is He, says: "Among My Friends, the one to be envied most, in My eyes, is the believer who has but little means and whose fortune is prayer, who worships his Lord in the best of modes, obeying Him in secret and in public. He is unnoticed among men; they do not point him out with their fingers. His livelihood is just sufficient, and he accepts that with patience."

Then the Prophet snapped his fingers and said:

His death is hastened, his mourners few, his estate of little worth.

FOURTH HADITH (4)

Anas [ibn Mālik] said:

One day when the Messenger of God, may God bless him and give him peace, was seated [amongst us], we saw him laugh and laugh until his teeth were showing. ʿUmar asked: "What makes you laugh, O Messenger of God, you for whom I would give my own father and mother?" He replied:

"Two men of my community were kneeling before the Lord of Might, ever exalted is He, and one of them said: 'O my Lord, retrieve for me what my brother has wrongfully taken from me!'

He said [to the accused]: 'Give back to your brother what you have wrongfully taken from him.'

'But my Lord,' he replied, 'nothing of merit has been left to me.'

'Then my Lord,' said [the first], 'let him carry some of my burden.'"

The eyes of the Messenger of God, may God give him blessings and peace, filled with tears, and he said: "Indeed that is a fearful day, when people will need someone to carry part of their burden." Then he continued:

"And God, ever mighty and majestic is He, said to the plaintiff: 'Raise your head and look towards the Gardens of Paradise.'

He raised his eyes and exclaimed: 'My Lord, I see cities of silver and palaces of gold, crowned with pearls. To which prophet or martyr does it belong?'

God replied: 'It belongs to whoever pays Me the price.'

He asked: 'And who, my Lord, will own it?'

God replied: 'You will.'

He asked: 'But how shall I do that, my Lord?'

God replied: 'By pardoning your brother.'

He said: 'My Lord, I have already pardoned him!'

God, ever exalted is He, said: 'Now take your brother by the hand, and lead him into Paradise.'"

Then the Messenger of God added:

"Fear God, and promote peace and reconciliation amongst yourselves, for surely God shall establish peace among the faithful on the Day of Resurrection."

FIFTH HADITH (5)

According to Abū Hurayra, the Messenger of God, may God give him blessings and peace, said:

When God created the Garden of Paradise and the Fire of Hell, he sent Gabriel to the Garden. He said: "Look upon it, and upon what I have made ready for its inhabitants."

So he went there and looked at what God had prepared for its inhabitants. When he returned, Gabriel declared: "By Your Might, anyone who hears of it will surely enter it!"

So God ordered Paradise to be veiled with unpleasant and hateful things, and said: "Return now and look upon what I have prepared for its occupants."

Gabriel returned to it, and beheld how it was veiled with hateful things. Then he came back to Him and declared: "By Your Might, I fear now that no-one will enter it!"

Then He said: "Go now to the Fire. Look upon it and upon what I have made ready for its inhabitants."

When he went there, Gabriel looked at it and at what had been prepared for its inhabitants. He saw how it was all piled up in layers, one on top of another. When he returned, Gabriel declared: "By Your Might, no-one who hears of it will enter it."

So God ordered the Fire to be encircled by pleasing and desirable things, and said: "Return now and look upon what I have prepared for its occupants."

Gabriel returned there and beheld how it was encircled by desires. Then he came back to Him and declared: "By Your Might, I fear now that no-one will be saved from entering it."

SIXTH HADITH (6)

Abū Bakr al-Ṣiddīq reported:

By God the Almighty, Muhammad, the chosen one, reported to me:
By God the Almighty, Gabriel, peace be upon him, reported to me:
By God the Almighty, Michael, peace be upon him, reported to me:
By God the Almighty, Israfil, peace be upon him, reported to me:

"God, ever exalted is He, says: 'O Israfil, by My Might and Majesty, by My Generosity and Liberality, for one who recites "In the name of God, the All-Compassionate, the Most Merciful" (*bismillāh al-raḥmān al-raḥīm*), followed immediately by the Fātiḥa of the Book just one time, you all bear witness that I have already forgiven him, that I have accepted his good deeds and set aside his evil deeds, that I shall not burn his tongue in the Fire, that I shall protect him from the punishment of the grave, from the punishment of Hell, from the punishment on the Day of Resurrection and from the Great Terror, and that he shall meet Me before all the Prophets and Saints.'"

SEVENTH HADITH (7)

According to Abū Hurayra, the Messenger of God, may God give him blessings and peace, said:

God, ever exalted is He, says: "The child of Adam slanders Me, but it is improper for him to slander Me. He accuses Me of lying, but it is improper for him to call Me a liar. As for slander, it is his claim that I have a son. As for accusing Me of lying, it is his assertion, 'He will not bring me back as He created me.' "

Abū Hurayra also reported these words of the Prophet, may God give him blessings and peace:

God, ever mighty and majestic is He, says: "The child of Adam accuses Me of lying, but that is not for him to do. He slanders Me, but that is not for him to do. As for accusing Me of lying, it is his assertion, 'He will not bring me back again as He created me before.' Yet the first creation was no more difficult for Me than his return will be. As for slandering Me, it is his claim, 'God has taken a son.' Yet I am the Unique One, the Eternal Refuge, I do not beget, nor am I begotten, and there is none like unto Me."[3]

EIGHTH HADITH (8)

According to Abū Hurayra, the Prophet, may God give him blessings and peace, said:

God, ever mighty and majestic is He, says: "O child of Adam, when you remember Me you are grateful to Me, and when you forget Me you are unfaithful to Me."

NINTH HADITH (9)

According to Abū Hurayra, the Prophet, may God give him blessings and peace, said:

God, ever mighty and majestic is He, says: "Provide [for others], and I shall provide for you."

Again he said:

The Hand of God is full. Its fullness is not diminished by constant provision, flowing night and day.

He added:

Have you not seen what He has provided since the creation of the Heavens and the Earth? Yet it has not diminished that which is in His Hand. His Throne is upon the water, and in His Hand is the Balance which rises or falls.

TENTH HADITH (10)

According to Abū Hurayra, the Messenger of God, may God give him blessings and peace, said:

God, ever mighty and majestic is He, says: "I am with My servant when he remembers Me and when his lips move in mention of Me."

ELEVENTH HADITH (11)

According to ʿAbdallāh ibn ʿUmar, the Prophet, may God give him blessings and peace, said:

Your Lord, ever mighty and majestic is He, says: "I shall not bring two fears together upon a servant, nor shall I bring together two securities upon him. If he fears Me in this world, he shall have no fear in the Other; and if he feels secure from Me in this world, then he shall have no security in the Other."

TWELFTH HADITH (12)

According to Abū Hurayra, the Messenger of God, may God give him blessings and peace, said:

God, ever mighty and majestic is He, shall say on the Day of Resurrection: "Where are those who have loved each other for the sake of My Majesty? Today I shall shelter them in My shade, on a day when there is no shade but My shade."

THIRTEENTH HADITH (13)

According to Abū Hurayra, the Messenger of God, may God give him blessings and peace, said:

God, ever mighty and majestic is He, says: "I am present in My servant's thought of Me, and I am with him when he beseeches Me."

FOURTEENTH HADITH (14)

According to Anas, the Prophet, may God give him blessings and peace, said:

God shall say to one of the People of the Fire who is enduring the lightest of punishments: "If you possessed everything on earth, would you then redeem yourself with it?"

To which he will reply: "Yes, I would."

Then He will say: "I asked of you something easier than that, when you were still in the loins of Adam: that you should not associate anything with Me. Yet you refused to do anything else but associate."

FIFTEENTH HADITH (15)

According to Abū Hurayra, the Messenger of God, may God give him blessings and peace, said:

God, ever mighty and majestic is He, says: "Pride (*kibriyā'*) is My cloak, and Grandeur (*'aẓama*) is My loincloth.[4] Whoever wrestles with Me over either of these, I shall cast him into the Fire."

SIXTEENTH HADITH (16)

According to Abū Sa'īd al-Khudrī, the Messenger of God, may God give him blessings and peace, said:

On the Day of Resurrection, God, ever mighty and majestic is He, shall say: "The angels have interceded, the prophets have interceded, the believers have interceded, and no-one remains except the Most Merciful of mercifiers."

Then, seizing a handful from the Fire, He will extract a group of mankind who have never done any good and who have been reduced to ashes. He will cast them into a river at the gates of Paradise, called the River of Life.

It continues:

Then God, ever glorified and exalted is He, will say: "Enter into Paradise. Whatever you see is yours."

They will reply: "Our Lord, You have given us something which You have not given to any one else in all the universes."

He will say: "For you I have something yet more precious than that."

They will ask: "Our Lord, what thing could be more precious than that?"

To this He will reply: "My Good-Pleasure (*riḍā'*)! I shall never again be displeased with you."

SEVENTEENTH HADITH (17)

According to Jābir ibn ʿAbdallāh, who received it from the Prophet, may God give him blessings and peace, who received it from Gabriel, who received it from God:

God, ever mighty and majestic is He, says: "Indeed this is a religion with which I Myself am well-pleased. Nothing befits it but open-handed generosity and nobility of character. So honour it with these two whenever you follow it."

EIGHTEENTH HADITH (18)

According to Ṣuhayb, the Prophet, may God give him blessings and peace, said:

When the people of the Garden have entered the Garden, God, ever exalted is He, will say: "Do you want for anything more that I may give you?"

They will reply: "Have You not illumined our faces? Have you not caused us to enter the Garden and delivered us from the Fire?"

The Prophet continued:

Then He will lift the veil, for they cannot be given anything that they would love more than vision of their Lord, ever mighty and majestic is He.

Then he recited this verse:

"The best, and more besides, is destined for those who strive with excellence."[5]

NINETEENTH HADITH (19)

According to Abū Sa'īd al-Khudrī, the Prophet, may God give him blessings and peace, said:

On the Day of Resurrection, God will say: "O Adam!"

He will reply: "Here am I, Lord, at Your service."

A voice will proclaim: "God commands you to extract from your progeny a contingent destined for the Fire."

Adam will ask: "Lord, what may be the contingent destined for the Fire?"

"From every thousand, nine hundred and ninety-nine, or thereabouts.[6] 'Thereupon the pregnant shall miscarry, the young shall become white-haired [with age] and you shall see men acting drunkenly. They will not be drunk, but indeed God's punishment is terrible.' "[7]

This made such a frightening impression on the people that their faces went pale.

The Prophet, may God give him blessings and peace, then added:

Descending from the people of Gog and Magog there shall be nine hundred and ninety-nine, whilst from among you only one. Among men you shall be like black hair on the flank of a white bull, or white hair on the flank of a black bull. Indeed I hope you will make up a quarter of the inhabitants of Paradise.

At this we exclaimed "*Allāhu akbar*!", and then he said: "One-third of the people of Paradise."

At this we exclaimed "*Allāhu akbar*!", and he said: "One-half of the people of Paradise."

Again we exclaimed "*Allāhu akbar*!"

TWENTIETH HADITH (20)

According to Ibn 'Abbās, the Messenger of God, may God give him blessings and peace, said:

God, ever mighty and majestic is He, revealed to Moses:

"There is no approach you can make to Me which I love more than [your] satisfaction with My decree. And there is no action you can perform which better preserves your good deeds than looking to your own affairs.

"O Moses, do not make requests of people of this world, lest I become displeased with you. And do not be generous with your religion (*dīn*) for the sake of this world, lest I close the doors of My Mercy to you.

"O Moses, say to the believers who have turned to Me in repentance: 'Rejoice.' And say to the believers who stand humbled before Me: 'Refrain from bad' or 'Do good.' "

The Shaykh adds: "The uncertainty is mine [as to which of these two injunctions is the correct reading]."[8]

TWENTY-FIRST HADITH (21)

According to Abū Hurayra, the Messenger of God, may God give him blessings and peace, said:

God, ever mighty and majestic is He, says: "For My righteous servants I have prepared what no eye has seen, nor ear heard, nor has entered into a human heart."[9]

TWENTY-SECOND HADITH (22)

According to ʿAlī ibn Abī Ṭālib, the Messenger of God, may God give him blessings and peace, said:

God, ever mighty and majestic is He, says:
"He who hopes for other than Me does not know Me.
"He who does not know Me does not worship Me.
"He who does not worship Me has incurred My Displeasure.
"He who fears other than Me, My Vengeance befalls him."

TWENTY-THIRD HADITH (23)

According to Abū Hurayra, the Messenger of God, may God give him blessings and peace, said whilst relating a ḥadīth concerning the final judgement of the servants on the Day of Resurrection:

One man remains, whose face is turned towards the Fire. He will be the last of the people of Paradise to enter Paradise. He cries: "O my Lord, avert my face from the Fire, for its stench tortures me and its heat consumes me." He continues to beseech God for as long as He wishes him to.

Then God, ever blessed and exalted is He, will say: "If I granted you this, would you ask anything else of Me?"

"No, I shall ask nothing else," he replies, and he makes whatever commitments and pledges to his Lord, ever mighty and majestic is He, that God wants him to make. Then God averts his face from the Fire.

When he comes towards Paradise and sees it, he keeps silent as God would wish, but then he will cry: "O my Lord, bring me up to the gate of Paradise!"

God, ever mighty and majestic is He, will reply: "Did you not make a commitment? Did you not pledge that you would ask nothing else of Me other than that which I have already given to you? Woe betide you, child of Adam, how faithless you are!"

The man replies "O my Lord!", and he beseeches God, ever mighty and majestic is He, until He says: "And will you ask anything else of Me if I grant it to you?"

"No, by Your Might!" Then he makes whatever commitments and pledges God wants him to make, and God brings him up to the gate of Paradise.

When he stands at the gate of Paradise, Paradise itself is opened out for him, and he will see all the wonderful delights therein. He keeps silent as God would wish, but then he will cry: "O my Lord, let me into Paradise!"

God, ever blessed and exalted is He, will reply: "Did you not make a commitment? Did you not pledge that you would ask for nothing other than that which you have been given? Woe betide you, child of Adam, how faithless you are!"

The man replies: "O my Lord, do not make me the most miserable of Your creatures!", and he will not cease to entreat Him until God, ever blessed and exalted is He, laughs at him.

And when God laughs at him, He will say: "Enter into Paradise."

Once he is there, God, ever exalted is He, will say: "Make a wish." He will ask his Lord and make a wish, with God reminding him of this and that, until all the wishes come to an end. Then God, ever mighty and majestic is He, will declare: "You shall have all that and more besides!"

TWENTY-FOURTH HADITH (24)

According to Abū Hurayra, the Messenger of God, may God give him blessings and peace, said:

When God created Adam and breathed into him the spirit, Adam sneezed and said "Praise be to God!",[10] and he praised Him with His permission.

His Lord replied: "May God have mercy on you, O Adam!"

Then he went to a group of angels who were sitting together, and said to them: "Peace be upon you!" They replied to him: "And upon you be peace and the mercy of God!"

Then he returned to his Lord, who said to him: "This shall be your greeting and the greeting of your children to each other."

Then God said, keeping His two Hands closed: "Choose whichever you will!"

"I choose the Right Hand of my Lord, and both Hands of my Lord are Right and Blessed."

Thereupon God opened it, and there were Adam and his progeny.

"My Lord, who are they?", Adam asked.

"These are your progeny", God replied.

Each human being had the duration of their life inscribed between their eyes. There was among them a man with a light more radiant than the others, or [at least] one of the most radiant.

Adam asked: "My Lord, who is he?"

"That is your son David, to whom I have assigned forty years of life."

"My Lord, prolong the duration of his life!"

"But that is what I have ordained for him."

"But Lord, I have already committed myself to giving him sixty years of my own term."

He replied: "You have, so be it."

The Prophet continued:

Then he stayed in Paradise as long as God willed, after which he was cast down. Adam himself kept account of his years, and then the Angel of Death came to him. Adam said: "You have come too soon. A thousand years were ordained for me."

"Indeed," replied the angel, "but you gave sixty of your years to your son David."

Adam denied, and his progeny denied. He forgot, and his progeny forgot.

The Prophet added that, since that day, written proof and witnesses have been made compulsory.

TWENTY-FIFTH HADITH (25)

According to Anas ibn Mālik, the Prophet, may God give him blessings and peace, said:

When God created the Earth, she began to quake. So He created the mountains and said to them: "Upon her", and she then became still.

The angels were amazed at the power of the mountains,[11] and they asked: "O Lord, is there anything in Your Creation more powerful than the mountains?"

He replied: "Yes, iron."

"O Lord, is there anything in Your Creation more powerful than iron?"

He replied: "Yes, fire."

"O Lord, is there anything in Your Creation more powerful than fire?"

He replied: "Yes, water."

"O Lord, is there anything in Your Creation more powerful than water?"

He replied: "Yes, wind."

"O Lord, is there anything in Your Creation more powerful than wind?"

"Yes, the child of Adam, who gives charitably with his right hand whilst concealing it from his left hand."

TWENTY-SIXTH HADITH (26)

According to Abū Hurayra, the Messenger of God, may God give him blessings and peace, spoke about the Day of Gathering, within which [the following appears]:

And there remains that community with its unbelievers amongst them. God, ever blessed and exalted is He, appears to them in a form different to that form of His which they recognise, and says: "I am your Lord!"

"We take refuge in God from you", they reply. "This is where we shall be until our Lord, ever mighty and majestic is He, comes to us. And when our Lord comes to us, we will know Him."

God, ever blessed and exalted is He, then comes to them in that form of His which they recognise, and says: "I am your Lord!"

"You are our Lord indeed!", they call out. They follow Him, and the path is laid down.[12]

This ḥadīth also mentions that God says:

"He who has worshipped a thing [other than Me] shall follow it."

TWENTY-SEVENTH HADITH (27)

According to Abū Hurayra, the Messenger of God, may God give him blessings and peace, said:

God, ever mighty and majestic is He, says:

"I am present in My servant's thought of Me, and I am with him when he remembers Me.

"If he mentions Me in his self, I mention him in My Self, and if he mentions Me in an assembly, I mention him in a better assembly than that.

"If he approaches Me by a hand's breadth, I draw near to him by an arm's length; and if he draws near to Me by an arm's length, I draw near to him by a fathom. If he comes to Me walking, I come to him running."

TWENTY-EIGHTH HADITH (28)

According to Anas ibn Mālik, the Messenger of God, may God give him blessings and peace, said:

God, ever mighty and majestic is He, says:

"O child of Adam, as long as you beseech Me and hope for Me, I shall forgive you whatever you have done, without minding in the slightest.

"O child of Adam, were your sins to reach up to the clouds of Heaven and then you asked forgiveness of Me, I should forgive you, without minding in the slightest.

"O child of Adam, even if you were to bring Me enough sins to fill the earth, but then you met Me without associating anything with Me, I should bring to you the selfsame measure of forgiveness."

TWENTY-NINTH HADITH (29)

Zayd ibn Khālid al-Juhanī reported that the Messenger of God, may God give him blessings and peace, performed the early morning prayer in our company at Ḥudaybiya,[13] after it had rained during the night. When he had finished, he turned towards the people and asked: "Do you know what your Lord has said?" They replied: "God and His Messenger know best." He said:

[God] says: "Two of My servants arise in the morning – one who believes in Me and one who does not believe in Me. As for the one who says, 'It has rained by the Blessing and Mercy of God', this one believes in Me and not in the stars. As for the one who says 'It has rained because of such-and-such a star', that one does not believe in Me but believes in the stars."

THIRTIETH HADITH (30)

Abū Mūsā al-Ash'arī reported a ḥadīth in which it is mentioned that the Messenger of God, may God give him blessings and peace, said:

And when the imam says [during the prayer]: "God hears him who praises Him", then say: "O God, our Lord, to You be praise!" so that God hears you. For indeed God, ever blessed and exalted is He, said through the mouth of His Prophet: "God hears him who praises Him."

THIRTY-FIRST HADITH (31)

Abū Hurayra said: I heard the Messenger of God, may God give him blessings and peace, say:

God, ever mighty and majestic is He, says: "I have divided the Prayer[14] into two halves between Me and My servant, and My servant shall have that for which he asks."

When the servant says: "Praise be to God, Lord of the universes", God says: "My servant has praised Me."

When he says: "The All-Compassionate, the Most Merciful", God says: "My servant has repeated My praises."[15]

When he says: "Sovereign King of the Day of Judgement", God says: "My servant has glorified Me" – *and once the Prophet said* – "My servant has given himself over to Me."

When he says: "It is You whom we adore and You whom we ask for help", God says: "This is between Me and My servant, and My servant shall have that for which he asks."

When he says: "Guide us along the straight path, the path of those to whom You have bestowed Your Favour, not of those who have incurred wrath, nor of those who go astray", God says: "This belongs to My servant, and My servant shall have that for which he asks."

THIRTY-SECOND HADITH (32)

When questioned about purity (ikhlāṣ), Ḥudhayfa said:

I asked the Messenger of God about purity and he said:

I asked Gabriel about it and he said: "I asked the Lord of Might concerning purity, and He replied: 'Secret of My secret, which I entrust to the heart of the one whom I love among My servants.'"

THIRTY-THIRD HADITH (33)

Muʿādh ibn Jabal reported:

I heard the Messenger of God say:

God, ever mighty and majestic is He, says: "Those who love one another in My Majesty shall have a raised dais (*manābir*)[16] of light which will be the envy of prophets and martyrs."

THIRTY-FOURTH HADITH (34)

According to Anas ibn Mālik, the Messenger of God, may God give him blessings and peace, said:

God says: "If I deprive My servant of his two eyes in this lower world, I shall give him in compensation nothing less than Paradise."

THIRTY-FIFTH HADITH (35)

According to Abū Hurayra, the Messenger of God, may God give him blessings and peace, said:

There will emerge, at the end of time, men who deceive the world through religion. They will dress up for men in sheep's clothing to display meekness, and their tongues will be sweeter than honey, but their hearts will be the hearts of wolves. And God will say:

"Are they trying to deceive Me, or are they acting insolently towards Me? By Me, I swear I shall send upon these people such a trial as will leave even the mildest-tempered (*ḥalīm*) of them in utter confusion."

THIRTY-SIXTH HADITH (36)

According to Anas, the Prophet, may God give him blessings and peace, said:

On the Day of Resurrection, the child of Adam will arrive like a lamb and stand before God, who will say to him:

"I gave you gifts, I furnished you with good, I bestowed favours upon you – and what have you done?"

He will reply: "I have gathered them up, I have made them multiply, and I have left them more abundant than before. Let me return [to the world] and I shall bring them to You."

Then God will say: "Show Me what you have brought out."

He will reply: "My Lord, I have gathered it up, I have made it multiply, and I have left it more abundant than before. Let me return and I shall bring it to you."

And if a servant does not bring out anything good, he will be sent to the Fire.

THIRTY-SEVENTH HADITH (37)

According to Abū Hurayra, the Messenger of God, may God give him blessings and peace, said concerning the Day of Resurrection:

I shall cry: "My community, O Lord! My community, O Lord! My community, O Lord!"

God will reply: "O Muhammad, bring in those of your community who have nothing to account for through the Right Gate of the Gates of Paradise. They are the equals of other men [who will enter Paradise] with respect to the other Gates."

THIRTY-EIGHTH HADITH (38)

'Abd al-Raḥmān ibn 'Awf reported:

I entered the mosque and I saw the Messenger of God leaving. I followed him, walking after him without him noticing me. Shortly afterwards he went into a palm-grove, turned towards the *qibla* and prostrated. His prostration lasted such a long time as I waited behind him that I began to wonder if God had caused him to die. So I approached him and bent down to look at his face. He raised his head and said: "What is the matter, 'Abd al-Raḥmān?"

"O Messenger of God," I replied, "when you made such a long prostration, I feared that God, ever mighty and majestic is He, had taken your soul, and so I came to look."

The Prophet declared: "When you saw me enter the palm-grove I met Gabriel, upon him peace, who said to me:

'I bring you tidings of joy: God, ever exalted is He, says to you: "He who greets you with peace, him shall I greet with peace. He who blesses you, him shall I bless."'"

THIRTY-NINTH HADITH (39)

According to Abū Hurayra, the Prophet, may God give him blessings and peace, said:

God, ever exalted is He, says: "O child of Adam, devote yourself exclusively to My worship, and I shall fill your breast with riches and preserve you from poverty. If you do not do this, I shall fill your hands with labour, and preserve you not from poverty."

FORTIETH HADITH (40)

Abū Sa'īd al-Khudrī and Abū Hurayra both testify that the Prophet, may God give him blessings and peace, said:

Whoever says: "There is no god but God" and "God is greater", his Lord confirms his truthfulness and says: "There is no god but Me" and "I am the Great."

And if he says: "There is no god but God alone", God says: "There is no god but Me alone."

And if he says: "There is no god but God alone; He has no partner", God says: "There is no god but Me alone, and I have no partner."

And if he says: "There is no god except God; His is the Kingdom and His the Praise", God says: "There is no god but Me; Mine is the Kingdom, and Mine the praise."

And if he says: "There is no god but God, and there is no power nor strength save through God", God says: "There is no god but Me, and there is no power nor strength save through Me."

The Prophet used to say: "Whoever says this in his illness and then dies, him the Fire shall not consume."

The servant who is in utter need of God, Muḥammad ibn ʿAlī ibn Muḥammad ibn al-ʿArabī, may God forgive him and his parents, his brothers, his companions and all muslims, says:

The forty *ḥadīth* are completed according to what I have recorded, may God give ease and the best of help by means of them, together with, as I mentioned, chains of transmission going directly back to God the High. Most of them I have collected from my companions, and I have transmitted them on the authority of the teacher from whom they themselves received them. In so doing, I wished to mention their place in the transmission of the Revelation, that they may also be placed in the line of the knowers of *ḥadīth* of the Messenger of God, may God's blessing and peace be upon him.

I shall now proceed to cite forty traditions going back to God but without chains of transmission.

PART TWO

IN THE NAME OF GOD,
THE ALL-COMPASSIONATE, THE MOST MERCIFUL

O my Lord! Make this easy through the blessing of Your Prophet, upon him be blessings and peace!

FIRST KHABAR (41)

God, ever mighty and majestic is He, said to His Prophet and Intimate Friend Abraham, upon him be peace: "What is this terrible fear you have?"

Abraham replied: "O my Lord, how should I not suffer fear and dread when my father Adam, may God bless him and give him peace, was in closeness with You; You created him with Your own Hand, and breathed into him of Your own Spirit; You commanded the angels to prostrate themselves before him; and yet, for a single act of disobedience, You cast him from Your Proximity?"

Then God inspired him thus: "O Abraham, do you not know how hard disobedience against the Beloved is for the Beloved?"

This tradition which I have transmitted goes back to Ibrāhīm ibn ʿAbdallāh, and appears in the book "The Degrees of Those Who Repent" (Kitāb Darajāt al-Tāʾibīn) by Ismāʿīl ibn Ibrāhīm al-Harawī, may God be pleased with him.

SECOND KHABAR (42)

God, ever exalted is He, said: "O David, caution the children of Israel against eating out of desire, for when the heart is attached to desire, the mind is veiled from Me."

This tradition which I have transmitted goes back to Abū Ja'far al-Jazarī and appears in the Darajāt al-Tā'ibīn by Ismā'īl ibn Ibrāhīm al-Harawī.

THIRD KHABAR (43)

God, ever exalted is He, said to Moses, upon him peace, when he asked Him: "O Lord, are You distant that I should call out to You? Or are You near that I should confide in You?":

"I keep company with him who remembers Me, and I am with him."

Moses asked: "What is the work You love most, O Lord?"

He replied: "That you propagate My Remembrance in every state."

This tradition which I have transmitted goes back to al-Maqburī and appears in the above-mentioned book.

FOURTH KHABAR (44)

God, ever exalted is He, says:

"He who pretends to love Me and neglects Me is a liar. Does not every lover seek to be secluded with his beloved?

"I am He who is completely aware of My lovers when they picture Me before them, address Me in contemplation and speak to Me in My Presence.

"Tomorrow I shall make their eyes delight in My Gardens."[1]

This tradition which I have transmitted goes back to al-Fuḍayl and appears in the above-mentioned book.

FIFTH KHABAR (45)

God, ever exalted is He, says concerning one who kills himself: "My servant has hastened to Me by his own doing; I have forbidden him Paradise."

This tradition which I have transmitted has an isnād going back to the Prophet, God's blessing and peace be upon him, which Muslim gives in his Ṣaḥīḥ.

SIXTH KHABAR (46)

God, ever mighty and majestic is He, says: "My true servant is the one who is in remembrance of Me when he faces his enemy."

This tradition which I have transmitted has an isnād going back to the Prophet, God's blessing and peace be upon him, in the collection of al-Tirmidhī.

SEVENTH KHABAR (47)

God, ever mighty and majestic is He, says:
"Indeed My Mercy and Compassion prevail over My Anger."

This tradition which I have transmitted has an isnād going back to the Prophet, God's blessing and peace be upon him, which al-Tirmidhī reported, commenting "With His own Hand He has prescribed [this Mercy] for Himself."[2]

EIGHTH KHABAR (48)

God, ever mighty and majestic is He, says:

"O child of Adam, if you are content with what I have apportioned you, you give ease to your heart and your body, and you will be praiseworthy.

"But if you are not content with what I have apportioned you, I shall subjugate you to this lower world to such a degree that you will gallop around like a wild animal in the open desert. By My Might and My Majesty, you will only obtain from the world what I have decreed for you, and you will be blameworthy."

This tradition which I have transmitted goes back to Ka'b al-Aḥbār[3] from the collection of al-Raba'ī,[4] who says it was taken from the Torah.

NINTH KHABAR (49)

God, ever mighty and majestic is He, says He will address the people of Paradise when they enter it: "Peace be upon you, My servants! Welcome. May God vivify you. Peace be upon you."

This tradition which I have transmitted has an isnād going back to the Prophet, God's blessing and peace be upon him, and comes from the ḥadīth of the "Abodes of the Resurrection" (Mawāqif al-qiyāma), reported by al-Naqqāsh.[5]

TENTH KHABAR (50)

God, ever mighty and majestic is He, says: "O child of Adam, each one wants you for himself, and I want you for yourself, yet you flee from Me. O child of Adam, how you wrong Me!"

This tradition which I have transmitted goes back to Kaʿb al-Aḥbār, and appears in the collection of al-Rabaʿī, who says it was taken from the Torah.

ELEVENTH KHABAR (51)

God, ever mighty and majestic is He, will say to one who was most well-off among the people of this world, when He immerses him in the Fire: "O child of Adam, have you ever seen any good? Have you ever experienced any pleasure?"

He will reply: "By God, no, my Lord!"

And then He, glory to Him, will say to one who was in the most wretched circumstances among the people of this world, when He immerses him in Paradise: "O child of Adam, have you ever seen any wretchedness? Have you ever suffered any hardship?"

He will reply: "By God, no, my Lord. I have never suffered any wretchedness, nor seen any hardship."

This tradition which I have transmitted has an isnād and appears in the collection of Muslim.

TWELFTH KHABAR (52)

God, ever mighty and majestic is He, says: "O child of Adam, I created you of dust, then of sperm, and your creation cost Me no effort. So how then should it cost Me to provide you with bread at any moment?"

This tradition which I have transmitted goes back to Ka'b al-Aḥbār and appears in the collection of al-Raba'ī, who says it is found in the Torah.

THIRTEENTH KHABAR (53)

God, ever mighty and majestic is He, says: "Peace be upon you from the All-Compassionate, the Most Merciful, the Living, the Self-Subsisting. You have been good, so enter into Paradise forever, for Paradise will be good for you. Let your souls find goodness in constant Munificence, in the reward of the Generous One, and in permanent abiding."

I have transmitted this tradition according to the ḥadīth of al-Naqqāsh.

FOURTEENTH KHABAR (54)

God, ever mighty and majestic is He, says: "O child of Adam, it is your right from Me that I be a lover for you. So, by My right from you, be for Me a lover."

This tradition which I have transmitted goes back to Kaʿb al-Aḥbār, may God be satisfied with him.

FIFTEENTH KHABAR (55)

God, ever mighty and majestic is He, will say in addressing the people of Paradise: "You are the faithful who rest in security, and I am God the Faithful who bestows security.[6] I have broken open for you a Name from among My Names. There shall be no fear for you, nor shall you be sad. You are My Friends, My Neighbours, My Beloved, My Chosen, My special ones, the people of My Love, and you are in My Abode."

This tradition which I have transmitted is from the ḥadīth of al-Naqqāsh in the Mawāqif [al-qiyāma].

SIXTEENTH KHABAR (56)

God, ever mighty and majestic is He, says, when He descends during the third part of the night: "I am the King! Who is there that calls out to Me, that I may answer him? Who is there that asks of Me, that I may give to him? Who is there that asks pardon of Me, that I may forgive him?"

This tradition which I have transmitted appears in the Ṣaḥīḥ of Muslim ibn al-Ḥajjāj.

SEVENTEENTH KHABAR (57)

God, ever mighty and majestic is He, says: "If My servant intends a good deed, then I count it for him as a good deed, even if he does not carry it out. And if he does carry it out, then I count it for him as ten like unto it. And if he plans to do an evil deed, then I forgive him for it, as long as he does not carry it out. And if he carries it out, I count it for him as it is."

I have transmitted this tradition according to the Ṣaḥīḥ of Muslim ibn al-Ḥajjāj.

EIGHTEENTH KHABAR (58)

God, ever mighty and majestic is He, says: "O child of Adam, I have created you for My sake, and I have created things for your sake. So do not disgrace that which I created for Myself with that which I created for you."

This tradition which I have transmitted goes back to Ka'b al-Aḥbār and appears in the collection of al-Raba'ī.

NINETEENTH KHABAR (59)

God, ever mighty and majestic is He, says: "O child of Adam, just as I do not make demands on you regarding what you will do tomorrow, so do not make demands on Me regarding [your] provisions for the morrow."

This tradition which I have transmitted goes back to Ka'b al-Aḥbār and appears in the collection of al-Raba'ī.

TWENTIETH KHABAR (60)

God, ever mighty and majestic is He, will say in addressing the people of Paradise: "Peace be upon you, O community of My servants who have surrendered [to Me]. You are the surrendered, and I am Peace.[7] My Abode is the Abode of Peace. I shall show you My Face as you have listened to My Word."

This tradition which I have transmitted appears in the Mawāqif of al-Naqqāsh.

TWENTY-FIRST KHABAR (61)

God, ever mighty and majestic is He, says: "O child of Adam, you owe Me obligations, and I owe you nourishment. Even if you betray Me in [your] obligations to Me, I shall not betray you in [My] nourishing of you, whatever you may have done."

This tradition which I have transmitted goes back to Ka'b al-Aḥbār and appears in the collection of al-Raba'ī.

TWENTY-SECOND KHABAR (62)

God, ever mighty and majestic is He, says: "O child of Adam, perform four prostrations in your prayer (*rakaʿāt*) at the beginning of the day, and I shall suffice you until the end of it."

This tradition which has an isnād I have transmitted according to the book of al-Nasāʾī, may God have mercy on him and be pleased with him.[8]

TWENTY-THIRD KHABAR (63)

God, ever mighty and majestic is He, says: "O child of Adam, how can you deem Me weak, when I have created you in this fashion? Despite My shaping you and proportioning you,[9] you strut about proudly, making the earth shake with your noise; you amass and you withhold, until you reach the point of death. Then you say: 'I will give in charity', but is that the time for charity?"

I have transmitted this tradition according to the ḥadīth of Asad ibn Mūsā.[10]

TWENTY-FOURTH KHABAR (64)

[God, ever mighty and majestic is He, says:]

"O child of Adam, if you give generously of the surplus you have, that is good for you, but if you withhold it, that is bad for you. You will not face reproach for having a sufficiency, and I shall take over with whoever you have to look after. The highest hand is better than the lowest."

I have transmitted this tradition from the Ṣaḥīḥ of Muslim ibn al-Ḥajjāj. He did not mention the following:

God, ever mighty and majestic is He, says: "If My servant has lost his state of purity and does not make an ablution, he maltreats Me. If he makes an ablution and does not pray, he maltreats Me. If he prays and does not then call to Me, he maltreats Me. If he calls to Me and I were not to respond to him, I would maltreat him. But I am not a Lord who commits maltreatment."

This tradition which I have transmitted comes from 'Abdallāh ibn Khamīs al-Kinānī, known as al-Jarrāḥ.[11]

TWENTY-FIFTH KHABAR (65)

God, ever mighty and majestic is He, says: "O child of Adam, do not fear for lack of nourishment, for My treasuries are full, and they shall never be exhausted."

This tradition which I have transmitted appears in the collection of al-Raba'ī.

TWENTY-SIXTH KHABAR (66)

God, ever mighty and majestic is He, will address the people of Paradise with the words: "When I reveal Myself to you, and I raise the veils from My Face, praise Me. Enter into My Abode in peace and security, veiled from Me no longer."

I have transmitted this tradition from the collection of al-Rabaʿī, according to the ḥadīth of al-Naqqāsh.

TWENTY-SEVENTH KHABAR (67)

God, ever mighty and majestic is He, says: "O child of Adam, have no fear of one who holds power, when My Power endures permanently. My Power is permanent, and it shall never be depleted."

I have transmitted this tradition according to the collection of al-Rabaʿī.

TWENTY-EIGHTH KHABAR (68)

God, ever mighty and majestic is He, says: "O child of Adam, you shall not be safe from My ruse until you have traversed the Path."

And God, ever exalted is He, says: "No-one, except those who are lost, feels safe from the ruse of God."[12]

I have transmitted this tradition according to al-Rabaʿī.

TWENTY-NINTH KHABAR (69)

God, ever mighty and majestic is He, will address the people of Paradise with the following words: "Come back to Me and sit down around Me, so that you may look upon Me and behold Me from near at hand. I shall gift you with My Gifts and I shall reward you with My Rewards. I shall surround you in My Light, and I shall envelop you in My Beauty. And I shall give you gifts from My Kingdom."

I have transmitted this tradition from the ḥadīth in the Mawāqif by al-Naqqāsh.

THIRTIETH KHABAR (70)

God, ever exalted is He, says: "I accept the prayer of one who humbles himself before My Grandeur, who does not seek to dominate My Creation, who does not pass a night persisting in disobedience of Me, who devotes his day to My Remembrance, who is merciful to the poor, the homeless, the widowed and to all who suffer misfortune. The light of such a one is like the light of the sun. I shall preserve him by My Might, and My angels will protect him. I shall provide him with light where there is darkness, and forbearance where there is ignorance. His likeness among My creatures resembles the Highest Garden in Paradise."

I have transmitted this tradition according to the collection of al-Bazzār.[13]

THIRTY-FIRST KHABAR (71)

God, ever mighty and majestic is He, says (when the angels say: "O Lord, there is a servant here who wants to commit an evil act" – and God knows better about it than they): "Watch over him, and if he performs it, reckon it to him as it is. And if he does not perform it, then reckon it to him as a good deed. For truly, he only abandons it for My sake."

I have transmitted this tradition according to the Sharḥ al-sunna of al-Baghawī.[14] *Muslim reports it as well.*

THIRTY-SECOND KHABAR (72)

On the Day of Resurrection, when actions are displayed, God, ever mighty and majestic is He, will say to the angels: "Look at the prayer of My servant and see if he has completed it or if he has omitted anything."

If he has completed it, it shall be set down as complete. If he has omitted anything in it, God will say: "See if My servant has done anything voluntarily."

He will declare: "Complete what My servant was required to do with what he did voluntarily."

The Prophet, may God give him blessings and peace, added: "It is thus that the works are accepted."

I have transmitted this tradition according to the "Book of Prayer" (Kitāb al-Ṣalāt), whose author imparted it to me during our meetings, may God have mercy upon him and illumine his face.[15]

THIRTY-THIRD KHABAR (73)

God, ever exalted is He, says: "O child of Adam, I strike you with three blows: poverty, illness, and death. And yet despite that, you are impetuous."

I have transmitted this tradition according to Mūsā ibn Muḥammad,[16] *who took it from 'Abd al-Wahhāb ibn Sukayna. Mūsā told me: "'Abd al-Wahhāb had it with an isnād going back to the Prophet, upon him be peace, who received it from God."*

THIRTY-FOURTH KHABAR (74)

God, ever mighty and majestic is He, answers someone who embarks upon the pilgrimage with unlawful possessions, saying "Here am I, Lord, at Your service", and says:

"There is no 'here am I, at Your service', until you have cast aside what you have in your hands."

I have transmitted this tradition according to a group of knowledgeable people, from whom I heard it without isnād or authority or ascription, may God be satisfied with them all.

God, ever exalted is He, said to Moses, upon him be peace:

"I shall teach you five sayings which constitute the pillars of Religion.

"Until you have learned that My Kingdom has ended, do not abandon your obedience to Me.

"Until you have learned that My Treasuries are exhausted, do not be concerned for your nourishment.

"Until you have learned that your enemy is dead, do not think yourself safe from attack, and do not neglect to fight.

"Until you have learned that I have forgiven you, do not criticise sinners.

"Until you have entered My Paradise, do not think yourself safe from My ruse."

This tradition was reported to us by Yūnus b. Yaḥyā in a chain of transmission going back through Jarīr to the Prophet.[17]

THIRTY-FIFTH KHABAR (75)

Giving the choice to His Prophet, may God give him blessings and peace, God, ever mighty and majestic is He, said: "You may be either prophet–servant or prophet–king. It is as you wish."

Gabriel, upon him be peace, revealed to him: "Be humble," and the Prophet, may God give him blessings and peace, replied: "Let me be prophet–servant."

I have transmitted this tradition according to the Darajāt al-Tā'ibīn by Ismā'īl al-Harawī, may God have mercy on him.

THIRTY-SIXTH KHABAR (76)

God, ever mighty and majestic is He, says: "Whoever demeans one of My Saints has declared war on Me."

I have transmitted this tradition according to the Darajāt al-Tā'ibīn and others.

THIRTY-SEVENTH KHABAR (77)

God, ever mighty and majestic is He, says: "The act of worship that is most beloved to Me is the giving of good counsel."

I have transmitted this tradition according to the "Darajāt al-tā'ibīn wa-maqāmāt al-qāṣidīn" by al-Harawī.

THIRTY-EIGHTH KHABAR (78)

God, ever mighty and majestic is He, will say in addressing the people of Paradise:

"I am your Lord whom you worshipped although you did not see Me. You called to Me, you loved Me, you feared Me.

"By My Might and My Majesty! By My Height and My Grandeur! By My Splendour and My Glory! Truly, I am well-pleased with you, I love you and I love what you love.

"You have in Me that which your souls desire and that which delights your eyes. You have in Me that which you ask for and that which you wish. All that you wish, I wish, so ask Me. Do not be shy or reticent."

I have transmitted this tradition according to the ḥadīth of the Mawāqif by al-Naqqāsh.

THIRTY-NINTH KHABAR (79)

God, ever exalted is He, says: "The child of Adam wrongs Me when he curses the time, for I am Time! In My Hand is the Order. I cause the night and day to turn, one upon the other."

I have transmitted this tradition following the Ṣaḥīḥ of al-Bukhārī.

FORTIETH KHABAR (80)

God, ever mighty and majestic is He, says to the angels on the Day of *'Arafa*:[18] "Regard My Servants! They come to Me dishevelled, dust-covered, down every long mountain-road. I call you all to witness that I have forgiven them."

The angels will then ask: "But Lord, this one has done wrong, and this one and that one!"

God, ever exalted is He, will reply: "I have already forgiven them."

I have transmitted this tradition following the book by Qāsim ibn Aṣbagh.[19]

The servant who is in utter need of God says:

Here end the forty traditions which go back to God without full chains of transmission, as I have recorded. We shall follow them with twenty *ḥadīth* going back to God with the chains of transmission of the books from which I have extracted them, rather than [producing] my own chains for them, for the sake of brevity. It was my wish that the whole work should comprise one hundred *ḥadīth*, to which I have added one more, in order to ensure an odd number. For: "God is Odd (*witr*) and loves the odd."

Here ends the second part, and praise be to God, Lord of the universes, and may He bless and grant peace to our master Muhammad, the unlettered prophet, and to his family and all his companions. May they be greeted with great peace.

PART THREE

IN THE NAME OF GOD,
THE ALL-COMPASSIONATE, THE MOST MERCIFUL

May God bless and grant peace to our master Muhammad, and his family and his companions.

FIRST HADITH (81)

The Messenger of God, may God give him blessings and peace, said:

God, ever mighty and majestic is He, has pledged Himself to him who goes forth [to fight] for His sake: "I shall not make him go forth to fight except for My sake, having faith in Me and believing in the veracity of My Messengers. I have guaranteed him that he will enter Paradise, or return to the home which he has left, after having received reward or booty."

Reported by Muslim, according to Abū Hurayra.

Then [the Prophet], upon him be peace, said:

And by Him who holds the soul of Muhammad in His Hand, there is no wound received for the sake of God except that [the victim] will appear on the Day of Resurrection in the condition he was in when he was wounded. His colour will be that of blood and his odour that of musk. And by Him who holds the soul of Muhammad in His Hand, if it were not burdensome for the Muslims, I would never remain behind when a contingent goes forth to fight for the sake of God, except that I would find no capacity to carry them [if they were wounded], nor would they find the capacity [to carry me], and it would be burdensome for them to remain behind after me.

By Him who holds the soul of Muhammad in His Hand, I would love to go forth and fight for the sake of God and be killed, fight again and be killed, fight again and be killed!

SECOND HADITH (82)

The Messenger of God, may God give him blessings and peace, said:

Our Lord, ever blessed and exalted is He, wonders at a man who goes forth to fight for the sake of God and then, when he is put to flight with his companions and he knows what his situation is, returns until his blood is shed. God says then to His angels: "Behold My servant! He returned out of desire and love for that which is with Me, until his blood was shed."

Reported by Abū Dā'ūd,[1] according to 'Abdallāh ibn Mas'ūd.

THIRD HADITH (83)

The Messenger of God, may God give him blessings and peace, said:

A man of the people of Paradise shall be brought forward, and God will ask: "O child of Adam, how do you find your abode?"

He will reply: "My Lord, it is the best of abodes."

God will say: "Ask and it shall be granted."

The man will reply: "I ask that You send me back to the world to be killed ten times over for Your sake." For he will have seen the bounty apportioned to the martyr.

Reported by al-Nasā'ī, according to Anas.

FOURTH HADITH (84)

The Messenger of God, may God give him blessings and peace, said:

Indeed God has angels who roam the roads, seeking out the people of Invocation (*dhikr*). When they find a group invoking God, they call out: "Come hither to what you have been looking for!" And they surround them with their wings, reaching up to the lowest heaven.

Their Lord questions them (yet He knows better than they): "What do My servants say?"

They reply: "They glorify and magnify You; they praise You and repeat Your praises."

He asks: "Have they seen Me?"

They reply: "No, by God, they have not seen You."

Then He asks: "And how would it be if they were to see Me?"

They reply: "If they were to see You, they would be stronger in service to You, stronger in repeating Your praises, and more profuse in glorifying You."

He asks: "What do they ask of Me?"

They reply: "They ask You for Paradise."

He asks: "And have they seen it?"

They reply: "No, O Lord, by God, they have not seen it."

Then He asks: "And how would it be if they were to see it?"

They reply: "If they were to see it, they would be stronger in striving for it, stronger in seeking it, and greater in their desire for it."

He asks: "Then from what do they seek refuge?"

They reply: "From the Fire."

He asks: "And have they seen it?"

They reply: "No, O Lord, by God, they have not seen it."

Then He asks: "And how would it be if they were to see it?"

They reply: "They would be faster in their flight from it and greater in their fear of it."

He says: "I call you all to witness that I have forgiven them."

But one angel will say: "Among them is so-and-so who is not one of them, for he only came out of need."

God will reply: "They are the sitting-companions. No-one who sits with them can be unhappy."

Reported by al-Bukhārī, according to Abū Hurayra.

FIFTH HADITH (85)

The Messenger of God, may God give him blessings and peace, said:

Moses, upon him be peace, said, "O Lord, teach me something by which I can invoke You and pray to You."

God replied, "O Moses, say: There is no god but God!"

Moses said, "O Lord, all Your servants say this."

He replied, "Say: There is no god but God!"

Moses said, "There is no god except You! And yet still I desire something that You give specially to me."

He replied, "O Moses, if the seven heavens and their inhabitants, and also the seven earths, were put in one of the scales [of the Balance of the Last Judgement], and 'There is no god but God!' was put in the other, 'There is no god but God!' would prevail."

Reported by al-Nasā'ī, according to Abū Sa'īd al-Khudrī.

SIXTH HADITH (86)

The Messenger of God, may God give him blessings and peace, said:

The angel [Gabriel] came to me and said: "O Muhammad, your Lord, ever mighty and majestic is He, says: 'Are you not satisfied with the fact that no-one prays over you without My praying ten times over him, and that no-one greets you without My greeting him ten times?'"

Reported by al-Nasāʾī, according to ʿAbdallāh ibn Abī Talḥa, according to his father, who reported: "The Messenger of God, God bless him and give him peace, came one day with a joyful face and we said to him: 'We see good news in your face.'"

Then he reported the ḥadīth which we have mentioned.

SEVENTH HADITH (87)

The Messenger of God, may God give him blessings and peace, said:

God created the creation, and when He had completed it, the tie of [blood] kinship arose and said: "This is the place where people seek refuge against all enmity amongst relatives."

[God] replied: "Yes. Are you not satisfied that I will attach those who come near to you in kinship, and that I will cut off those who go against you in enmity?"

It replied: "Indeed."

[God] said: "Then that is yours."

Then the Messenger of God, may God give him blessings and peace, said:

Recite, if you wish: "Would you not then, if you turned away, create disorder on the earth and sever your ties of kinship? They are the ones whom God curses, so that He makes them deaf and blinds their sight. Will they not ponder on the Qur'an or is it that there are locks upon their hearts?"[2]

Collected by Muslim, according to Abū Hurayra.

EIGHTH HADITH (88)

The Messenger of God, may God give him blessings and peace, said:

God, ever blessed and exalted is He, says: "My love is by necessity for those who love one another in Me, for those who sit with one another in Me, for those who give generously to one another in Me, and for those who visit one another in Me."

Reported by Mālik ibn Anas, according to Mu'ādh.

NINTH HADITH (89)

The Messenger of God, may God give him blessings and peace, said:

When God loves a servant, he calls Gabriel and says to him: "Indeed, I love so-and-so, so love him!" So Gabriel loves him, and then calls forth in heaven: "Indeed, God loves so-and-so, so love him!"

Then the inhabitants of heaven love him, and after that, acceptance is accorded him on earth.

When God loathes a servant, He calls Gabriel and says: "Indeed, I loathe so-and-so, so loathe him!" So Gabriel loathes him, then announces to the inhabitants of heaven: "Indeed, God loathes so-and-so, so loathe him!"

Then they loathe him, and after that, loathing is accorded him on earth.

Reported by Muslim, according to Abū Hurayra.

TENTH HADITH (90)

God, ever mighty and majestic is He, said:

A servant commits a sin and says: "O God! Forgive me my sin!"

Then He, ever blessed and exalted is He, says: "My servant has committed a sin. He knows that he has a Lord who forgives sin and takes it [from him]."

After that he sins again and says: "O my Lord, forgive me my sin!"

Then He, ever blessed and exalted is He, says: "My servant has committed a sin. He knows that he has a Lord who forgives sin and takes it [from him]."

After that he sins again and says: "O my Lord, forgive me my sin!"

Then God, ever blessed and exalted is He, says: "My servant has committed a sin. He knows that he has a Lord who forgives sin and takes it [from him]. Do what you will for I have already forgiven you."

Reported by Muslim, according to Abū Hurayra.

ELEVENTH HADITH (91)

The Messenger of God, may God give him blessings and peace, said:

God, ever blessed and exalted is He, says: "Whoever treats a friend of Mine as an enemy, on him I declare war. My servant draws near to Me by nothing dearer to Me than that which I have established as a duty for him. And My servant does not cease to approach Me through supererogatory acts until I love him. And when I love him, I become his hearing with which he hears, his sight with which he sees, his hand with which he grasps, and his foot with which he walks. And if he asks Me [for something], I give it to him. If he seeks refuge with Me, I place him under My protection. In nothing do I hesitate so much as I hesitate [to take] the soul of a believer. He has a horror of death, and I have a horror of harming him."

Reported by al-Bukhārī, according to Abū Hurayra.

TWELFTH HADITH (92)

The Messenger of God, may God give him blessings and peace, said:

On the Day of Resurrection there will be sealed scrolls placed before God. He will say to the angels: "Reject this and accept that." Then the angels will say: "By Your Might, we have seen nothing but good."

The Most High – and He is more knowing – will say: "That was done for other than Me, and today I only accept such deeds as were done to seek My Face."

Reported by al-Dāraquṭnī[3] in his Sunan, according to Anas ibn Mālik.

THIRTEENTH HADITH (93)

The Messenger of God, may God give him blessings and peace, said:

God, ever mighty and majestic is He, says to this world: "O world, serve the one who serves Me, and wear out the one who serves you."

Reported by 'Abd al-Ḥaqq[4] in his Raqā'iq, according to 'Abdallāh ibn Mas'ūd.

FOURTEENTH HADITH (94)

God, ever glorified and exalted is He, says: "Any servant whose body I preserve in health and whose livelihood I enlarge with plenty, should he pass five years without coming to Me, he will be debarred."

Reported by Abū Bakr b. Abū Shayba, according to Abū Sa'īd al-Khudrī.

FIFTEENTH HADITH (95)

The Messenger of God, may God give him blessings and peace, said:

On the Day of Resurrection, God shall redeem one man from my community above all the creatures. Ninety-nine scrolls [on which his sins are recorded] shall be unrolled before him, each scroll stretching as far as the eye can see.

Then He will ask: "Do you contest anything among all that? Have the guardian angels been unjust to you?"

[The man] will reply: "No, my Lord! I do not contest any of it."

[God] will say: "Have you any argument in your defence?"

[The man] will reply: "No, my Lord!"

[God] will then say: "Indeed, you have a good deed with Us! There shall be no injustice wrought upon you today."

And a sheet of paper shall be produced on which is written: "I bear witness that there is no god but God, and I bear witness that Muhammad is His servant and His messenger."

[God] will say: "Bring your scales!"

[The man] will ask: "My Lord, what is this sheet [of paper] in relation to those scrolls?"

[God] will reply: "Truly, you shall not be wronged."

Then the scrolls will be placed in one of the scales, and the sheet of paper in the other. The scrolls will appear to be lighter and the sheet of paper will weigh heavily. For nothing has weight in relation to the Name of God, ever mighty and majestic is He.

Reported by al-Tirmidhī, according to ʿAbdallāh ibn ʿAmr ibn al-ʿĀṣ.

SIXTEENTH HADITH (96)

The Messenger of God, may God give him blessings and peace, said:

The angels will assemble before God and bear witness in favour of the servant for the pure deeds which he has performed for God.

God will say: "You are the guardians of My servant's deeds, but I am the Watcher over that which is in his heart. In truth, he did not intend Me by that act; he desired other than Me, so My curse is upon him."

Reported by Ibn al-Mubārak, according to Muʿādh ibn Jabal, who said: "I heard the Messenger of God, may God give him blessings and peace, say to me ..." and he reported the ḥadīth concerning the bringing-out of acts, which is a long one, and we have reported it in its entirety in our Arbaʿīn al-Ṭiwāl,[5] without omitting anything which has come down to us.

SEVENTEENTH HADITH (97)

The Messenger of God, may God give him blessings and peace, said:

There are three kinds of people whose requests are never rejected: he who fasts until his fast is broken, the imam who is just, and he who has suffered oppression.

God raises up their request towards Him beyond the clouds, and opens the gates of Heaven for it. The Lord then says: "By My Might, I shall indeed help you, even though it may take a while."

Reported by al-Tirmidhī, according to Abū Hurayra.

EIGHTEENTH HADITH (98)

The Prophet of God, may God give him blessings and peace, explained with regard to God's saying: "On the day when We shall call all men with their leader (*imām*)"[6]:

One of them will be called, and he will be given his book in his right hand. He will have his body extended by 60 cubits, and his face will be graced with light, and upon his head will be placed a crown of shimmering pearl. When he goes off to his companions, they will see him coming from far away, and cry out: "O God, grant us such as this, and give us such a blessing."

Then He grants it to them, saying: "Rejoice! For each one of you shall have the like of this."

As for the man without faith, his face will turn black, and he will have his body extended by 60 cubits according to the form of Adam.

He will wear a crown of fire, and when his companions catch sight of him, they will call out: "We take refuge in God from the evil of this. O God, do not give us this."

Then He gives it to them, and they say: "O God, please delay it a while."

He replies: "God has banished you. Each one of you shall have the like of this."

The Prophet of God, may God give him blessings and peace, said:

This is bestowed upon the servant on the Day of Resurrection: He asks him: "Did I not give you hearing and sight, wealth and children? Did I not give you power over cattle, and leave you to manage and pasture them? And did you once think that you were going to meet Me on this your day?"

He will reply: "No."

Then God will add: "Today I shall forget you just as you forgot Me."

Reported by al-Tirmidhī, according to Abū Hurayra.

God, ever mighty and majestic is He, will say on the Day of Resurrection,

"O child of Adam, I was sick, and you did not visit Me."

[The man] asks: "My Lord, how could I visit You, when You are the Lord of the universes?"

He will reply: "Did you not know that one of My servants was sick, and you did not visit him? Did you not know that if you had visited him, you would have found Me with him?"

"O child of Adam, I asked you for food, but you did not feed Me."

[The man] asks: "My Lord, how could I feed You, when You are the Lord of the universes?"

He will reply: "Did you not know that one of My servants asked you for food, and you did not feed him? Did you not know that if you had fed him, you would have found that with Me?"

"O child of Adam, I asked you for drink, but you gave Me nothing to drink."

[The man] asks: "My Lord, how could I give you a drink, when You are the Lord of the universes?"

He will reply: "One of My servants asked you for drink but you did not quench his thirst. Did you not know that if you had quenched his thirst, you would have found that with Me?"

Reported by Muslim, according to Abū Hurayra.

NINETEENTH HADITH (99)

Abū Hurayra reported: "The Messenger of God, may God give him blessings and peace, told me:"

When the Day of Resurrection comes, God will descend to the servants to judge between them. Each community will be kneeling. The first one to be called will be a man who collected the Qur'an, and then will come a man who was killed [in battle] for the sake of God, and then a wealthy man.

God asks the Qur'an reciter: "Did I not teach you that which I brought down [by inspiration] upon My Messenger?"

[The man] replies: "Certainly, my Lord."

[God] will ask: "And what did you do with what you learned?"

He will reply: "I practised it night and day."

[God] will say to him: "You are lying."

And the angels will say: "You are lying."

God will say: "You [did all that] so that it might be said 'So-and-so is a reciter.' And that is what was said."

The wealthy man will be brought next. God asks him: "Did I not provide for you so generously that I did not let you be in need of anyone?"

[The man] replies: "Certainly, my Lord."

[God] will ask: "And what did you do with what I gave you?"

He will reply: "I strengthened the bonds of kinship and gave alms."

[God] will say to him: "You are lying."

And the angels will say: "You are lying."

God will say: "You [did all that] so that it might be said 'So-and-so is generous.' And that is what was said."

Then the one who was killed for the sake of God will be brought and God asks him: "Under what circumstances were you killed?"

[The man] replies: "You ordered us to fight for Your sake, so I fought until I was killed."

God will then say to him: "You are lying."

And the angels will say: "You are lying."

God will say: "You [did all that] so that it might be said 'So-and-so is courageous.' And that is what was said."

The Messenger of God, may God give him blessings and peace, then slapped Abū Hurayra on the knee and said: "O Abū Hurayra, these three will be the first of God's creation for whom the fire will be kindled on the Day of Resurrection."

Reported by al-Tirmidhī, according to Abū Hurayra.

TWENTIETH HADITH (100)

The Messenger of God, may God give him blessings and peace, said:

By Him who holds my soul in His Hand, you shall come to no harm in seeing your Lord.

God will meet with the servant and ask, "O so-and-so, tell Me: was I not generous towards you, did I not give you authority, did I not grant you a wife, did I not give you power over horses and camels, did I not put you in charge and grant you a quarter [of the spoils of war]?"

The man will reply: "Indeed, my Lord!"

God will ask: "And did you once think that you were going to meet Me?"

[The man] will reply: "O Lord, I have believed in You and in Your Book and in Your Messengers, I have prayed, fasted and given alms", and he will repeat God's praises in the best way he is able to.

When he has spoken, God will say: "Come here now."

Then it will be said to him: "We have just dispatched Our witness against you."

The man will wonder to himself: "Who is it that will testify against me?"

Then a seal will be put over his mouth, and it will be said to his legs: "Speak!"

Thereupon his legs, his flesh and his bones will speak of his actions, making apology for his soul.

That is the hypocrite. That is he with whom God is displeased.

Reported by Muslim, according to Abū Hurayra, who said: "The Companions asked: 'O Messenger of God, will we see our Lord?' Then [the Prophet] mentioned the ḥadīth relating to the Vision and quoted this."

TWENTY-FIRST HADITH (101)

This is the one hundred and first divine ḥadīth, and with it the book is completed.

The Messenger of God, may God give him blessings and peace, said:

In Paradise, God, ever exalted is He, says to the people of Paradise:

"I am God, the One who gives lavishly, the Rich beyond need, the One who fulfils His promises perfectly, the wholly Truthful. This is My Abode, and I have let you dwell here. This is My Garden, and I have granted you complete access to it. This is My Self, and I have let you see Me. Here is My Hand which holds the dew and the rain, generously spread out over you, without ever being kept from you. And I, I gaze upon you, without ever turning My Eyes away from you. So ask Me whatever you wish and desire.

"I have made you intimate with Myself. I am the One who is sitting with you, delighting in your company. Never more shall there be need or want, suffering or misery, weakness or old age, discontent or oppression, nor shall this ever be changed for all eternity.

"The bounty of Eternity is your felicity. You are those who rest in security, and permanently abide in eternal existence, the ennobled, the blessed! You are the most noble lords, who have been obedient to Me and have avoided My prohibitions. So bring your needs to Me. Let Me satisfy them for you, with generosity and munificence."

They reply: "Our Lord, it is not this that we hoped and longed for. What we want of You is the sight of Your Generous Face for all eternity, and Your good-pleasure with us."

Then the High, the Supreme, the King of the kingdom, the One who gives most lavishly and generously, ever blessed and exalted is He, says to them:

"This is My Face, which discloses Itself to you forever and ever. Rejoice, for I Myself am well-pleased with you. Enjoy! Go to your spouses, embrace them and celebrate your marriage. [Go] to your newborn [daughters] and play with them. [Go] to your chambers and enter them. Go to your gardens and stroll in them. [Go] to your mounts and ride them. [Go] to your beds and lie down upon them. [Go] to your slave-girls and concubines in the garden [of Paradise] and be intimate with them. [Go] to the gifts bestowed by your Lord and receive them. [Go] to your clothing and wear it. [Go] to your meetings and be in conversation.

"Then rest awhile, without slumber or fear of attack, within the shelter of the shade, in peace and tranquillity, in the proximity of the Majestic One. Retire to the river Kawthar,[7] to Kāfūr,[8] to the Pure Water,[9] to Tasnīm[10] and Salsabīl and Zanjabīl. Bathe there and take your delight, be blessed and may you have a good return.

"Then go and be seated upon the green cushions and beautiful carpets,[11] on raised couches in pools of shade, with trickling water and abundant fruits, unfailing and unrestricted."[12]

Then the Messenger of God, may God give him blessings and peace, recited:

"Indeed the inhabitants of Paradise shall be taken up with joy on that day, they and their spouses, resting in the shade on couches. They shall have the fruits of happiness and all that they request: Peace, as a word of a Merciful Lord."[13]

Then he recited this other verse:

"The inhabitants of Paradise that day shall possess the better dwelling-place and the fairer resting-place."[14]

This ḥadīth was reported to me several times by the Shaykh, the Imam, scion of the Prophet, transmitter of ḥadīth, Abū Muḥammad Yūnus b. Yaḥyā b. Abū al-Ḥasan b. Abū al-Barakāt b. Aḥmad b. ʿAbdallāh b. Muḥammad b. Aḥmad b. Ḥamza b. Ismāʿīl b. Muḥammad b. ʿĪsā b. Mūsā b. Muḥammad b. ʿAlī b. ʿAbdallāh b. al-ʿAbbās, uncle of the Messenger of God, may God give him blessings and peace!

Sometimes I read it aloud to him while he listened, and sometimes he read it to me while I listened, [and this was] in the interior of the Sacred Precinct (al-Ḥaram al-Sharīf) and facing the most venerated Kaʿba, in Jumāda al-ākhira of the year 599. He told me he had received it himself from the Qāḍī Abū al-Faḍl Muḥammad b. ʿUmar b. Yūsuf al-Urmawī, from Abū Bakr Muḥammad b. ʿAlī b. Muḥammad known as Ibn Khayyāṭ, from Abū Sahl Maḥmūd b. ʿUmar al-ʿUkbarī, from Abū Bakr Muḥammad b. al-Ḥasan al-Naqqāsh, from Abū Bakr b. al-Ḥusayn al-Ṭabarī al-Buzūrī, from Muḥammad b. Ḥumayd al-Rāzī, from Salama b. Ṣāliḥ, from Qāsim b. al-Ḥakam, from Salām al-Ṭawīl, from Ghiyāth b. al-Musayyab, from ʿAbd al-Raḥmān b. Ghanm and Zayd b. Wahb, from ʿAbdallāh b. Masʿūd. He recounted from ʿAlī the ḥadīth of "the Stations of the Resurrection" and from the Prophet the ḥadīth of "God's Address to the people of Paradise", which we have mentioned.

Here ends the book entitled "The Niche of Lights concerning some of the communications which have been transmitted from God, ever glorified is He". This third part was completed, and with it the whole work, in the Sacred Precinct of Mecca in the afternoon of Sunday, the third day of the month of Jumāda al-ākhira, in the year 599 [16 February 1203]. It was written in his own hand by its author, Muḥammad b. ʿAlī b. Muḥammad b. al-ʿArabī al-Ṭāʾī al-Ḥātimī. May God have mercy on the one who reads it, and may He bless the one who has written it.

And may God bless our master Muhammad, his family and his companions, and may He greet them all with peace.

O You, my surest confidence!
O You, my abiding hope!
May You seal my work with great good![15]

Notes to the translation

Part One

1. That is to say, if a needle were put into the sea and then withdrawn, the tiny drop of water adhering to the needle would not diminish the sea itself.
2. "But when [the sun] set [Abraham] said: 'O my people, surely I am quit of what you associate. I have turned my face to Him who originated the heavens and the earth, a man of pure faith; I am not of the idolaters'" (Q.6:78).
3. The final sentence is a personalised form of the Sūrat al-Ikhlāṣ (Q.112).
4. Another version of this *ḥadīth*, quoted by Ibn 'Arabī in the *Futūḥāt* (II.102–3), reads: "Exalted Might (*'izza*) is My loincloth, and Grandeur My cloak. Whoever contends with Me over either of these, I shall shatter him." See also the first lines of Psalm 93: "The Lord reigneth, He is clothed with majesty (pride); the Lord is clothed with strength (grandeur), wherewith He hath girded Himself."
5. Q.10:26.
6. Literally, "From every thousand" [Muhammad said:] I think He said: "Nine hundred and ninety-nine."
7. Q.22:2, describing the earthquake of the last Hour.
8. The Arabic words for these two injunctions would be very similar.
9. Compare with Isaiah 64:4: "Since ancient times no-one has heard, no ear has perceived, no eye has seen any god besides You, who acts on behalf of those who wait for Him;" and I Corinthians2:9: "No eye has seen, no ear has heard, no mind has conceived what God has prepared for those who love Him."
10. This is the basis for Ibn 'Arabī's description in the *Futūḥāt* (II.190): "When the Form of the Image revealed itself in the Mirror of the Essence, [the Creator] said to [the Adamic Form] – when [the latter] perceived [its likeness in the Mirror of] the Essence, and [the Form] *sneezed* and made its Self to stand out – 'Praise *whom you see*!' So [the Form] praised its *Self* and said: 'Praise belongs to God.' And [the Creator] said to [the Form]: 'May your Lord have mercy on you, O Adam! For this did I create you.'" (Translated by G. Elmore in "*Ḥamd al-ḥamd*: The Paradox of Praise in Ibn al-'Arabī's Doctrine of Oneness", in *Praise*, p.86.)
11. In some manuscripts this first section reads as follows:

When God created the Earth, it began to quake. Then the angels asked, "How, O Lord, will Your servants find stability upon this earth?" Whereupon He appeared to them in a revelation that caused them to swoon. When they came to, the angels saw that the mountains had been created.

12. In some manuscripts this reads: "the bridge over Hell is laid down".
13. A village on the edge of the Sacred Precinct of Mecca, where the Prophet led over a thousand pilgrims to make the pilgrimage in 7/628. He entered a special state of grace there, and all the Companions were commanded to pledge their allegiance to him. A peace treaty with Quraysh was then concluded, which guaranteed access to Mecca in future years.
14. This refers to the uttering of the Sūrat al-Fātiḥa in the ritual prayer.
15. The Arabic *athnā* means both "to double" and "to praise or extol".
16. The *minbar* (pl. *manābir*) was originally a raised platform or dais from which the Prophet addressed the community in Medina.

Part Two

1. Literally, "cool their eyes in My Gardens". This Arabic idiom denotes the pleasure that comes after the heat of the desert day, which makes the eyes red, and is also associated in another *ḥadīth* with the pleasure the Prophet experienced in prayer.
2. Some manuscripts report a different *ḥadīth qudsī* here:

   God, ever mighty and majestic is He, says: "O child of Adam, if only you were to see how little is left of your appointed time! You would renounce all expectations for the future, you would restrain your greed and your devising, and you would seek to augment [your good deeds]. Nonetheless, remorse shall seize you [at the moment of death], when your foot falters, when your family and servants desert you, when your dearest leaves you and your nearest forsake you. You will not be able to return to your people, nor add to what you have done. Work, then, in view of the Day of Resurrection, the day of sorrow and remorse."

   This tradition I have taken from revealed scriptures, in a chain of transmission from Yūnus b. Yaḥyā al-'Abbāsī, on the authority of Abū al-Futūḥ Muḥammad b. Muḥammad b. 'Alī alī-Ṭā'ī, on the authority of Salama b. Shabīb, on the authority of Manṣūr b. 'Umar, on the authority of his father, on the authority of Zakarīya b. Ibrāhīm, on the authority of Salama b. 'Abd al-Malik, on the authority of Wahb al-Munabbih.

   [Abū 'Abdallāh Wahb al-Munabbih al-Yamanī was born about twenty years after the Prophet's death, a famous Follower who listened to some of the Companions and related from them. He is celebrated for his Book of

Military Campaigns, describing the Prophet's battles, and as an authority on the traditions of the Jews and Christians. He died in 110/728.]

3. Ka'b al-Aḥbār was brought up as a Jew in the Yemen, and is reported to have been present at the Prophet's last sermon in Medina. He became Muslim in the time of Abū Bakr and was a companion to 'Umar. He was known for transmitting traditions regarding previous prophets such as Moses and Dhu'l-Kifl. He died in 32/652.
4. Abū Sulaymān Muḥammad b. 'Abdallāh al-Raba'ī, died 379/989.
5. Abū Bakr Muḥammad b. al-Ḥasan al-Naqqāsh (266–351/880–962), from Baghdad.
6. In Arabic, the word *mu'min* denotes both the one who has faith in God and a Divine Name, the One who gives the security of faith.
7. In Arabic, peace (*salām*) and the surrendered (*muslimūn*) are from the same etymological root.
8. Abū 'Abd al-Raḥmān b. Shu'ayb al-Nasā'ī (215–302/820–914) was born in Khorasan, and travelled widely in pursuit of *ḥadīth*, settling eventually in Egypt. In 302/914 he went to Damascus, where he composed a book on the merits of 'Alī, for which he was much criticised and driven out of the mosque. He compiled a huge *Sunan*, which contained a number of dubious traditions, and then a synopsis, *al-Mujtabā*, which is now accepted as one of the six canonical collections.
9. See Q.82:7: "O man, what has deceived you as to your generous Lord who created you and shaped you and proportioned you and composed you in whatever form He willed for you?"
10. Asad b. Mūsā al-Urmawī, known as Asad of the *Sunna*. A *muḥaddith*-sufi, he died in Egypt in 212/827.
11. One of Ibn 'Arabī's masters in the Maghrib, al-Kinānī had been a companion of Abū Madyan. He was a surgeon who lived just outside Tunis, and was buried in La Marsa. See Hirtenstein, *Unlimited Mercifier*, p.89.
12. Q.7:99.
13. Abū Bakr Aḥmad b. 'Amr al-Bazzār, a scholar from Basra who compiled two *ḥadīth* collections. He died in Ramla in 291/904.
14. Abū Muḥammad al-Ḥusayn b. Mas'ūd al-Farrā', known as the reviver of the *Sunna*. A native of Khorasan, al-Baghawī lived in Marw (Merv) and died there in 516/1122, aged over eighty. He was famed for his commentary on the Qur'an and the very complete collection of *ḥadīth* entitled *Sharḥ al-sunna*.
15. Presumably Muḥammad ibn Qassūm, who was Ibn 'Arabī's teacher and companion in Andalusia. See R.W.J. Austin, *Sufis of Andalusia*, p.83.
16. Probably Mūsā b. Muḥammad al-Qabbāb who is named as present at the reading of the *Rūḥ al-quds* in Mecca in AH600. See *Fut.* I. 603.
17. Jarīr b. 'Abdallāh was a close friend of Ibn 'Abbās (21–96/642–714).
18. A plain some 25km to the east of Mecca, where pilgrims gather for the central

ceremonies of the *Ḥajj* on the 9th Dhu'l-Ḥijja, the last month of the Muslim year. One of the main events is the halting in front of the Mountain of Mercy (*Jabal al-Raḥma*), a small rocky eminence in the valley itself. As is mentioned in the Qur'an, in the Divine Address to Abraham: "Proclaim among men the Pilgrimage, and they shall come to You on foot, upon every lean beast, proceeding from every mountain-road, that they may witness that which is beneficial for them and mention God's Name on days well-known over such beasts as He has provided them with. So eat thereof and feed the wretched poor" (Q.22:27–8).

19. Qāsim b. Aṣbagh al-Bayyānī (d.340/951).

Part Three

1. Abū Dā'ūd Sulaymān b. al-Ashʿath al-Sijistānī (203–275/817–889) was born in Khorasan, and received his main *ḥadīth* training in Basra, where he was to finally settle. He was well-known for his encyclopaedic knowledge and memory, as well as honesty and kindliness. His *Sunan* is one of the most celebrated books on *ḥadīth* and sacred law.
2. Q.47:23–5.
3. Abū al-Ḥasan ʿAlī b. ʿUmar (306–85/918–95) is generally known as al-Dāraquṭnī, because he lived in a part of Baghdad known as Dār al-Quṭn. He compiled several works on *ḥadīth*, in particular his *Sunan*, which was recognised as one of the most reliable collections.
4. ʿAbd al-Ḥaqq al-Azdī al-Ishbīlī, whom Ibn ʿArabī mentions at the beginning of his list of *ḥadīth* teachers in the *Ijāza* – see p.94.
5. This work of Ibn ʿArabī's on *ḥadīth* is mentioned in his *Fihrist* (no.31) and *Ijāza* (no.32). Its title indicates that it was a collection of longer *ḥadīth*, perhaps compiled in Mecca around the same time as the *Mishkāt*.
6. "… and whoever is given their book in their right hand, they shall read their book, and shall not be wronged in the slightest" (Q.17:70).
7. "To you We have given *al-kawthar*, pray to your Lord and sacrifice" (Q.108:1–2). *Al-kawthar* is usually taken to mean a river in Paradise or a pond which the Prophet saw near the zenith of his ascension (*miʿrāj*). According to a *ḥadīth* recorded by Ṭabarī (Tafsīr no.6), Muhammad arrived at a tree so vast as to give shade and shelter to the whole Islamic community, and at its foot was the source of two rivers: the river of Mercy and al-Kawthar. After bathing in the river of Mercy, Muhammad was allowed to cross Kawthar and enter Paradise. In another tradition, the water-source which feeds the other two rivers is named as Salsabīl. The mystical interpretation is founded on the connection with a word from the same Arabic root,

kathra (multiplicity): Kawthar thus refers to the vision of unity in multiplicity and multiplicity in unity.

8. "Surely the virtuous (*al-abrār*) shall drink of a cup flavoured with *kāfūr* (camphor), a fountain from which drink the servants of God, causing it to gush forth" (Q.76:5–6). Camphor was revered as a medicine and perfume. This Sura goes on to mention that they will also drink in Paradise "a cup flavoured with *zanjabīl* (ginger), therein a fountain whose name is Salsabīl" (Q.76:17–18).
9. "He it is who sends the winds as heralds of His Mercy, and We send down from the heaven pure water" (Q.25:48).
10. "Tasnīm, a fountain from which drink those brought close (*muqarrabūn*)" (Q.83:27).
11. Q.55:76.
12. Q.56:29–33.
13. Q.36:55–8.
14. Q.25:24.
15. This final prayer, which only appears in some manuscripts, seems to be taken from a *ḥadīth* transmitted by al-Naqqāsh. See *Mishkāt al-anwār*, Cairo, 1999, p.69.

Appendix

Ḥadīth and Ibn ʿArabī

Qur'an, ḥadīth and ḥadīth qudsī

In general, the Arabic word *ḥadīth* (plural *aḥādith*) means "news" or "report". As William Graham notes, "the word *ḥadīth* itself is impossible to render in English by one word that is satisfactory for all senses of the original. 'Tradition' is the usual translation, but this does not convey the inherent sense of *something spoken* or *narrated* that the Arabic root does."[1] As a technical term within Islam, a *ḥadīth* signifies a report of things said by the Prophet Muhammad, or a report of things which he did, or which he saw others do and tacitly accepted. Such *ḥadīth* are referred to as *ḥadīth nabawī* (or sometimes *ḥadīth sharīf*, translated as prophetic *ḥadīth*), reported by one of his close Companions.

In contrast, *ḥadīth qudsī* (or *ḥadīth ilāhī* or *rabbānī*, translated as Divine or Sacred Sayings) are a special kind of *ḥadīth*, reporting a communication spoken by God Himself to the Prophet Muhammad, who thus assumed the role of transmitter. On occasion, such *ḥadīth* are addressed by God to another prophet, such as Abraham, Moses or David, or to the angels, and reported by Muhammad. There are also several which God specifically addresses directly to the "children of Adam" (or "Son of Man") or people in the next world.[2]

Although both Qur'an and *ḥadīth qudsī* convey the word of God Himself, there are important distinctions to be made between them. For example, the Qur'an was revealed through the medium of Gabriel, and is inimitable; a *ḥadīth qudsī* does not necessarily come through Gabriel, but may be revealed through inspiration or a dream. While a Muslim must recite portions of the Qur'an during the prescribed prayers, it is not permitted to include *ḥadīth qudsī*. An important difference also arises in the way each has been preserved and transmitted. The Holy Book, the Qur'an, was revealed

1. See William Graham, *Divine Word and Prophetic Word in Early Islam*, p. 47 n. 108.
2. In the *Mishkāt*, for example, we find 5 *ḥadīth qudsī* addressed to Muhammad, 8 to other prophets, 12 to the angels, 18 to the child of Adam, and 20 to people in the next world (i.e. on the Day of Judgement, in Paradise, etc.).

to Muhammad (born AD 570) from his fortieth year. Parts of the Qur'an were uttered by Muhammad at different times during the course of twenty-three years, and on his instruction these were recorded by being committed to memory by many people, and by being written down. The first collection of the Qur'an seems to have been a written copy of the entire text in the reign of the first Caliph, Abū Bakr. The form of the Qur'an as we know it today resulted from the action of the third Caliph, ʿUthmān (ruled AD 644–56), who had all the existing records collected together and written down less than twenty years after the death of Muhammad. This definitive version, known as the Uthmanic codex, has remained essentially unchanged to the present day. Although there is a record of the existence of some variants prior to ʿUthmān's redaction, and there was some further development of the text when vowel-marks were added to it (AD 688), there is a virtually total consensus in traditional Islam about the authenticity and completeness of the Quranic text as we have it.

While some *ḥadīth* were memorised and indeed may have been written down during the life of Muhammad, this process was less systematic and organised than in the case of the Quranic revelation. The record of the Prophet's example conveyed by *ḥadīth*, which is called the *Sunna*, is fundamental to the life of Islam, as the natural complement to the Qur'an, and Muslims are encouraged to seek guidance from it in an effort to emulate Muhammad. The *ḥadīth* corpus was reported by the Companions, those who had enjoyed the privilege of having lived in the Prophet's company. It is upon their reliability and integrity that the trustworthiness of the huge number of *ḥadīth* collected by later generations of Muslim scholars rests. Of these Companions, only a small number took it upon themselves to report *ḥadīth*: the vast majority of the traditions which have come down to us are related by fewer than 300 Companions. A mere eleven are responsible for handing down more than 500 *ḥadīth* each. Seven of these Companions, each of whom reported more than 1,000 traditions, are known as the *mukaththirūn*, the narrators of many traditions;[3] all of them enjoyed a long association with the Prophet, had a tremendous interest in recording *ḥadīth* accurately, and could speak with great authority about what he had said and done. They all outlived the Prophet, and thus were able to pass on their knowledge to succeeding generations.

3. These seven are: Abū Hurayra (5374 traditions), ʿAbdallāh b. ʿUmar (2630), Anas b. Mālik (2286), ʿĀ'isha Umm al-mu'minīn (2210), ʿAbdallāh b. ʿAbbās (1660), Jābir b. ʿAbdallāh (1540) and Abū Saʿīd al-Khudrī (1170).

According to one well-known *ḥadīth*, the Prophet is reported to have said: "I have left two things among you. You will not go astray as long as you hold on to them: the Book of God and my *Sunna*." Nonetheless, the initiative to establish a definitive record of *ḥadīth* did not come to fruition until well over a hundred years after the death of Muhammad, and the six major collections which are regarded as the most authoritative by the Sunni community[4] were set down during the third century AH.

In the process of taking evidence from countless people who recounted what had come down to them from and about the Prophet, the men who made such collections (*muḥaddithūn*) developed a system of principles for assessing the trustworthiness of such accounts. The authenticity of a *ḥadīth* is assessed by the reliability of its reporters (*rāwī*) and the continuity of the links between them. Consequently the *isnād*, or list of the names of people who passed a *ḥadīth* on from one to another, forms an important part of a *ḥadīth* in its full form, as well as the actual text (*matn*) itself. For a number of reasons, the accounts which make up the *Sunna* are not all equally reliable, and a critical methodology has been developed to evaluate their relative authenticity, described in terms of strength or weakness. It is thus universally acknowledged that there is need for discretion in the case of *ḥadīth*, despite their importance, because of the way they have come down to us. However, the reader is fortunate that Muḥyīddīn Ibn ʿArabī is a guide of perfect taste and discernment, and a consummate *muḥaddith*.

Ḥadīth qudsī do not form a separate group within the major books of tradition. It appears to have been nearly five hundred years after the Prophet before the first collection was made solely of *ḥadīth qudsī*. At least, the earliest work cited by William Graham[5] is the *Kitāb al-aḥādith al-ilāhiyya* by Ẓāhir b. Ṭāhir al-Shahhāmī al-Naysābūrī (d. 533/1138), half a century before Ibn ʿArabī was born. Nonetheless, Ibn ʿArabī's *Mishkāt al-anwār* is the second oldest text of this kind mentioned by Graham, being completed in the year 599/1203. It is unusual in that it is not just drawn from the books of tradition, but also contains one section of forty *ḥadīth qudsī* with a full *isnād* for each, which begins from the people who transmitted the *ḥadīth* to Ibn ʿArabī. Other collections were made later by other authors from existing texts,

4. The six most authoritative Sunni collections are the two *Ṣaḥīḥ*s compiled by al-Bukhārī (d. 870) and Muslim ibn al-Ḥajjāj (d. 875), followed by the *Sunan* works of Abū Dā'ūd al-Sijistānī (d. 888), Abū ʿĪsā al-Tirmidhī (d. 892), Abū ʿAbd al-Raḥmān al-Nasā'ī (d. 915), and Ibn Māja al-Qazwīnī (d. 887). Some people, Ibn ʿArabī included, seem to have preferred Mālik's *Muwaṭṭa'* to the *Sunan* of Ibn Māja.

5. See Graham, *Divine Word*, Appendix I, for a chronological list of fifteen collections of Divine Sayings that exist in manuscript or printed form.

the largest comprising 858 traditions compiled by Muḥammad al-Madanī (d. 881/1476).

One of the characteristics of *ḥadīth qudsī* is that they might be described as "pithy sayings", that is to say, sayings whose few words contain a wealth of meaning. They embody the quality that the Prophet Muhammad referred to when he explained that he had been given the *jawāmi' al-kalim* (literally, the synthesis of the words).

Muḥyīddīn Ibn 'Arabī and ḥadīth

Born in Murcia in southern Spain (the Andalus of the Arabs) in 1165 (AH 560), Ibn 'Arabī began his study of *ḥadīth* in Seville at about the age of fifteen or sixteen, as the result of a remarkable spiritual experience. During a period of retreat he had a unique vision of the three major prophets of the Western tradition: Jesus, Moses and Muhammad, each of whom gave him particular instruction. In the vision, he was rescued from danger by the Prophet Muhammad, who said to him: "My beloved, hold fast to me and you will be safe." Ibn 'Arabī says, "It was from that time on that I occupied myself with the study of *ḥadīth*."[6]

It was as a result of this vision that he began his spiritual quest in earnest. Soon afterwards, he came into contact with several spiritual teachers in Andalusia, and rapidly displayed his exceptional gifts. In Cordoba in 1190 (AH 586), for example, he had a glorious vision of all the prophets, from Adam to Muhammad, during which he was told of his own function as Seal of Muhammadian Sainthood. As he says in a poem,

> Without doubt I am the heir of the knowledge of Muhammad
> And of his state, both secretly and manifestly ...[7]

Ibn 'Arabī left Spain to make the pilgrimage at the age of thirty-five. He arrived in Mecca in July or August 1202 (AH 598) and spent the next two and a half years there. During this period he had several visionary experiences, including an encounter with the mysterious youth, who he describes as a union of opposites, "steadfast in devotion, who is both speaker and silent, neither alive nor dead, both complex and simple, encompassed and encompassing". From

6. *Kitāb al-Mubashshirāt*, p. 5; Hirtenstein, *Unlimited Mercifier*, p. 55.
7. For further biographical details of this period, see Hirtenstein, *Unlimited Mercifier*, Chapters 3–7.

this meeting came the inspiration for the vast *Futūḥāt al-Makkiyya* (Meccan Illuminations), a 37-volume résumé and exposition of spiritual knowledge, encompassing all the dimensions of Islam, arranged in 560 chapters. The setting-down of the *Futūḥāt* took place over a period of nearly thirty years, during which time Ibn ʿArabī travelled over much of the Middle East, finally settling in Damascus. For the last eighteen years of his life, from 1223 to 1240 (AH 620–38), Ibn ʿArabī wrote and taught prolifically. He had hundreds of students drawn from all walks of religious and spiritual life. During this time in Damascus he completed his famous *Fuṣūṣ al-ḥikam* (Settings of Wisdom), a book presented to him in a dream by the Prophet himself. In it he summarised his teaching through an exposition of the spiritual message of each prophet, from Adam to Muhammad. He died at the age of seventy-five, and was buried in the Ṣāliḥiyya area of Damascus, just north of the city walls, and his shrine is still much-visited and revered today.[8]

Most modern scholars have written little about the place of *ḥadīth* in Ibn ʿArabī's life and writings. They have preferred instead to concentrate on the profundity of his thought, and show its connections to the Qur'an.[9] Yet it is quite clear from any investigation of his works that he cultivated the most thorough knowledge of the whole Islamic tradition, and he was known during his lifetime as a reliable transmitter of *ḥadīth*.[10]

Acknowledged as a profound writer on spiritual matters, and a teaching master in his own right, Ibn ʿArabī continued to study *ḥadīth* whenever he could throughout his life, eager to gain knowledge wherever it presented itself. It was during the middle part of his life, the two and a half years spent in Mecca, that he composed the *Mishkāt al-anwār*, and at least four other major works.[11] When he arrived in Mecca, he found himself amidst an extraordinary group of people:

> When I began my stay in Mecca in the year 598, I met there a group of most eminent men and women, the élite of good behaviour and

8. For full details of Ibn ʿArabī's life and thought, see Hirtenstein, *Unlimited Mercifier*, and Claude Addas, *Quest for the Red Sulphur*.

9. See, for example, the work of William Chittick, whose indexes also include Hadith, and Michel Chodkiewicz, in particular the latter's *An Ocean Without Shore*. James Morris has indicated the importance of *ḥadīth* in his article "Seeking God's Face".

10. For example, one of his disciples, Ayyūb b. Badr al-Muqri', normally refers to Ibn ʿArabī as "the master, imam, man of knowledge, transmitter of *ḥadīth*" (*al-shaykh al-imām al-ʿālim al-muḥaddith*). Details can be found in an unedited manuscript in the Süleymaniye library in Istanbul (Shehit Ali 2813).

11. The four books are *al-Mahajjat al-bayḍā'* (also dedicated to *ḥadīth*), *Ḥilyat al-Abdāl* (on the path to sainthood), *Tāj al-rasā'il* (a collection of love-letters addressed to the Kaʿba) and the *Rūḥ al-quds* (which includes stories of his masters in Andalusia).

> spiritual learning. Although they were all people of distinction, I saw none more concerned with self-knowledge, more enamoured of observing the daily changes in his state, than the learned shaykh, imam of the Station of Abraham (*maqām Ibrāhīm*), a native of Isfahan who had taken up residence in Mecca, Abū Shujā' Ẓāhir bin Rustem,[12] and his elderly and learned sister, lady of the Ḥijāz, Fakhr al-Nisā' bin Rustem.[13]

This particular man, Abū Shujā', was a noted *muḥaddith*, recounting to Ibn 'Arabī the *ḥadīth* of al-Tirmidhī. This information comes from Ibn 'Arabī's *Ijāza*, a bibliography of his own works which he wrote in later life. Here also we can find the names of those who passed on to him traditional *ḥadīth* disciplines and transmitted to him many compilations of *ḥadīth*, the most prominent being:

(1) 'Abd al-Ḥaqq al-Azdī al-Ishbīlī (of Seville) who transmitted to him all his works on *ḥadīth*. He lived in Bejaia (Bougie) in Algeria, and was a close friend of the famous Maghribi shaykh, Abū Madyan. He died in 581/1185.

(2) 'Abd al-Ṣamad al-Ḥarastānī, the *qāḍī* of Damascus, who transmitted to him Muslim's *Ṣaḥīḥ* in the Umayyad Mosque of the city. He died in 614/1217.

(3) Yūnus b. Yaḥyā al-'Abbāsī al-Ḥāshimī, who transmitted to him many works, including Bukhārī's *Ṣaḥīḥ*. A disciple of 'Abd al-Qādir al-Jīlānī, he is extremely prominent in the collection in the *Mishkāt al-anwār*, being named as the transmitter of no less than twenty *ḥadīth qudsī*. He died in 608/1211.

(4) Naṣr b. Abū Faraj al-Ḥāshimī, who transmitted to him many works, including Abū Dā'ūd's *Sunan* while he was in Mecca. He died in 619/1222.

There then follows a list of nearly sixty people whom Ibn 'Arabī recorded as his teachers in *ḥadīth* disciplines.

12. His daughter, Niẓām, was the inspiration for the writing of a beautiful collection of poems, *Tarjumān al-ashwāq* (Interpreter of Ardent Desires), translated by R. A. Nicholson.

13. *Tarjumān*, pp. 10–11; Hirtenstein, *Unlimited Mercifier*, p. 149.

Ibn 'Arabī's other ḥadīth writings

In his *Fihrist*, which catalogues 248 of his works written up to 627/1229, Ibn 'Arabī mentions several books dedicated to *ḥadīth* apart from the *Mishkāt al-anwār*. Most appear to be lost, and those that do remain have not been the subject of much study to date. The following selection will give an idea of the range and profusion of Ibn 'Arabī's writing:

(1) *K. al-Maḥajjat al-bayḍā' fī'l-aḥkām al-shar'iyya* (The Noble Path in performing the Divine Statutes) – this treatise on *fiqh* was composed in Mecca a year later than the *Mishkāt al-anwār*, and the second part, written in his own hand, formed part of his stepson al-Qūnawī's private library in Konya, Turkey.

(2) *K. Miftāḥ al-sa'āda* (The Key to true happiness) – he specifies that this work was a compilation of the collections of Muslim and Bukhārī, and some of Tirmidhī's *ḥadīth*. The autograph manuscript of part of Bukhārī's *Ṣaḥīḥ*, which is dedicated to al-Ḥabashī and held in the National Library of Tunis, may be part of this larger work.

(3) *K. al-Misbāḥ fī jam' bayn al-ṣiḥāḥ* (The Lamp of Light in the collection of sound traditions) – this appears to have been a synthesis of the six canonical collections, of Bukhārī, Muslim, Tirmidhī, Ibn Māja, Abū Dā'ūd and Nasā'ī.

(4) *K. Kanz al-abrār fīmā ruwiya 'an al-nabī min al-ad'iya wa'l-adhkār* (The Treasure of the virtuous regarding prayers and invocations which have been transmitted from the Prophet).

(5) *K. al-Arba'īn ḥadīthan al-mutaqābila wa'l-arba'īn al-ṭawīlāt* (The Book of forty *ḥadīth* of meeting and forty long *ḥadīth*) – this is quoted in the *Mishkāt al-anwār* as being already written.

(6) *K. Mishkāt al-ma'qūl al-muqtabasa min nūr al-manqūl* (The Niche of the rational, taken from the light of the traditional) – a work in nine chapters, contrasting rational and inspired gifts.

The Mishkāt al-anwār

The full title of the work is "The Niche of Lights concerning some of the communications which have been transmitted from God" (*Mishkāt al-anwār fīmā ruwiya 'an Allāh min al-akhbār*). The book, at least in title, is clearly inspired by the famous Light Verse (*āyat al-nūr*) in the Qur'an:

> God is the Light of the heavens and the earth; the likeness of His Light is as a niche wherein is a lamp, the lamp in a glass, the glass as it were a glittering star kindled from a blessed tree, an olive that is neither of the East nor of the West, whose oil would shine, even if no fire touched it; Light upon Light; God guides to His Light whoever He wishes. And God strikes similitudes for men, and God has knowledge of everything.[14]

The imagery of this verse has formed the basis for much contemplation within the Islamic tradition. In a *ḥadīth* reported by Ṭabarī:

> Ibn ʿAbbās [cousin of the Prophet] came to see Kaʿb al-Aḥbār and asked him: "Tell me about God's words 'the symbol of His Light is as a niche'", to which Kaʿb replied: "The niche is a hole in the wall which God has given as a symbol of Muhammad, blessings and peace be upon him; 'wherein is a lamp', the lamp designates his heart; 'the lamp in a glass', the glass is his chest …"[15]

According to Ibn ʿArabī's friend and teacher in Tunis, ʿAbd al-ʿAzīz al-Mahdawī, the "niche" (*mishkāt*) is the symbol of Muhammad's body, the "lamp" his heart, the "glass" his mind, the "star" his secret heart (*sirr*), "kindled from a tree" whose origin is light. Mahdawī also understood the verse in a macrocosmic sense, with the "niche" symbolising the Divine Throne (in other words the whole "body" of manifestation), the "lamp" the light of Muhammad and the "glass" the bodies of the prophets.[16] For Ibn ʿArabī himself, the "niche" also appears as an image of the external covering of the heart, a "cordial" membrane that gives protection against the passions (*ahwāʾ*), while the glass symbolises the heart which has attained the station of purity (*ṣafāʾ*) – its transparency allows the light of the heart's lamp to shine forth, finding its fullest degree in the person of the Prophet.[17] In the *Mishkāt al-anwār* the "lights" are the Divine Sayings which appear in the "niche" of the Prophet, who manifests the glory and beauty of these lights exactly as they are in reality.

Ibn ʿArabī's title for this collection of *ḥadīth qudsī* is reminiscent of another very well-known work, also entitled *Mishkāt al-anwār*, by the great twelfth-century theologian and mystic, Abū Ḥāmid al-Ghazālī (d. 505/1111).

14. Q.24:35.
15. *Jāmiʿ al-bayān*, XVIII, 104–11.
16. See P. Beneito and S. Hirtenstein, "The Prayer of Blessing by ʿAbd al-ʿAzīz al-Mahdawī".
17. See *Fut.* I. 434.

The two works are, however, quite different in approach: while Ghazālī is concerned with establishing a metaphysics of light, Ibn 'Arabī provides a work of great depth and simplicity by collecting together Divine Sayings.[18]

The *Mishkāt* is the only book in the vast body of Ibn 'Arabī's writings that is specifically dedicated to *ḥadīth qudsī*. As he explains at the beginning, he compiled this collection as a way of conforming to two *ḥadīth*:

> According to Ibn 'Abbās, the Messenger of God, may God give him blessings and peace, said: "Whoever preserves for my community forty *ḥadīth* of the *Sunna*, I shall be his intercessor on the Day of Resurrection." According to Anas ibn Mālik, the Messenger of God, may God bless him and give him peace, also said: "Whoever preserves for my community forty *ḥadīth* of which they stand in need, God shall put him down as learned and knowing."

He then explains that since man stands more in need of the other world than of this one, he will provide two collections of forty *ḥadīth* with a further section of twenty to make it up to one hundred, with an extra one to respect the Divine "Singleness" (*witr*). This again conforms to a well-known *ḥadīth*: "God is Odd/Single and loves the odd."

The 101 *ḥadīth* of the *Mishkāt al-anwār* thus fall into three sections. The first forty each have a full, unbroken chain of transmission which goes back to God through the medium of the Prophet Muhammad (*al-aḥādith al-musnada*). The second forty, entitled *khabar* (which means "news" or "information"), go back to God without a complete chain via the Prophet (*al-aḥādith al-marfū'a*), and are mostly taken from well-known collections such as those by Muslim or Tirmidhī. Seven of these are drawn from a long tradition on the Abodes of the Resurrection, reported by al-Naqqāsh (d. 351/962). The final section of twenty (*al-aḥādith al-mursala*) are drawn from similar books, with the last *ḥadīth* given a direct chain. This tripartite division explains why the work has come to be known under various titles.

At the end of the last section Ibn 'Arabī specifies when the *Mishkāt* was written down:

> This third part was completed, and with it the whole work, in the Sacred Precinct of Mecca in the afternoon of Sunday, the third day of the month of Jumāda al-ākhira, in the year 599 [16 February 1203].

18. Ghazālī's work is altogether more theoretical in nature, though based upon the same Quranic verse and the same principle of Muhammadian light: "If the heavenly lights from which the earthly lights become kindled have a hierarchy such that one light kindles another, then the light nearest the First Source is more worthy of the name 'light' because it is highest in level" (al-Ghazālī, *The Niche of Lights*, pp. 13–14).

The writings of Muḥyīddīn Ibn ʿArabī are inseparably infused with the words of the Qur'an and *ḥadīth*, and some *ḥadīth* in the *Mishkāt* appear prominently and frequently in his other works. For example, the thirty-first *ḥadīth*, concerning the three parts of the ritual prayer, is an important part of the Chapter of Muhammad in the *Fuṣūṣ al-ḥikam*. James Morris has drawn attention to those *ḥadīth qudsī* concerning the vision of the face of God. The 101st *ḥadīth* at the end of the *Mishkāt*, which Ibn ʿArabī studied while facing the Kaʿba, appears in full in Chapters 64 and 65 of the *Futūḥāt*.[19]

An interesting example of Ibn ʿArabī's use of this selection of *ḥadīth qudsī* is to be found at the very end of the enormous *Futūḥāt*, in Chapter 560. This final chapter describes the fundamental instruction which he gives to all who would lead the spiritual life, in a series of nearly 170 practical teachings (*waṣiyya*). In many ways a summary of what has come before in the *Futūḥāt*, these "reminders of what God has commanded" are taken from the Quran, Hadith, his own experience and the experience of other mystics. There are several sections that quote and sometimes comment upon *ḥadīth qudsī*, which in almost all cases are drawn directly from the *Mishkāt*. A close analysis shows that no less than 60 out of the 101 are repeated verbatim, in fact all those which particularly constitute advice to people in this world, rather than Divine addresses to people in Paradise. Although the overall organisation is different, two long passages (*Fut*. IV. 527–9 and 534–6) reiterate the precise order of the *Mishkāt al-anwār*, leading us to conclude that this latter was certainly used in the writing of the final chapter.

Further, in Chapter 560 Ibn ʿArabī sometimes adds comments upon the implications of these *ḥadīth*. One striking example is the first *ḥadīth qudsī* mentioned in the *Mishkāt*, which emphasises our utter dependence upon God for guidance, sustenance and forgiveness. This he describes as being "like a remedy for whatever sickness befalls certain weak souls with regard to the knowledge of God, when they have no knowledge of what is meant by His saying 'there is no thing like Him'." Telling his reader to apply these remedies, he adds: "If you neglect what I have advised you to do, you will have only yourself to blame. If you are ignorant, then I have informed you. If you are forgetful, then I have awakened you and reminded you. If you are a believer, then this reminder will benefit you. For myself, I have obeyed God's command in reminding you, and your making use of the reminder is testimony to your faith ... This is my instruction, so adhere to it, and this is my advice, so know it well."[20]

19. This *ḥadīth* is the final part of the tradition on the Abodes of the Resurrection, other parts of which are cited in *Khabars* 9, 13, 15, 20, 26, 29 and 38.

20. *Fut*. IV. 452.

It is true that in other works he quotes some *ḥadīth* and *ḥadīth qudsī* which have been disputed by scholars on the grounds that their historical chains of transmission are inadequate. An obvious example is the saying, "I was like a hidden treasure, and I loved to be known; so I created the world that I might be known." Ibn 'Arabī states that he knew this to be sound by spiritual unveiling.[21] However, he did not confuse one kind of knowledge with another, and *ḥadīth qudsī* of that kind are not included in this book.

Transmission and reception

In this translation the sayings are presented in the English translation in their simplest form. That is, the list of people involved in their transmission is reduced to the minimum in the text, so that the actual sense of the Divine Saying may be seen as clearly as possible. Many of these *ḥadīth* appear in collections that had been written down hundreds of years earlier, but for Ibn 'Arabī the process of receiving them was primarily through person-to-person communication.

Concerning the first collection of forty *ḥadīth*, Ibn 'Arabī says, "Most of them I have collected from my companions, and transmitted them on the authority of the teacher from whom they themselves received them." At the end of the first section, Ibn 'Arabī mentions that he has included in the lists of transmitters of the *ḥadīth* the names of those companions who related these *ḥadīth* to him, so that they might also be accounted "learned and knowing".

The chains of transmission (*isnād*) which Ibn 'Arabī gives are mainly found in the first section of forty *ḥadīth*. These *isnād*s provide the names of all those *muḥaddithūn* (transmitters) from whom Ibn 'Arabī personally received the *ḥadīth* in question, in a line that stretches back to the Prophet, the original transmitter from God. Eleven different contemporaries are mentioned as those who transmitted to him personally, although in fact two of them (marked below with an asterisk) did so only on the authority of the agency of another. These eleven direct links between Ibn 'Arabī and the rest of the chain can for the most part be identified, and a brief biographical sketch is given here for each of them. The numbers in brackets refer to the number of the *ḥadīth* in the text of the *Mishkāt*, where the name of the transmitter in question appears.

21. This *ḥadīth*, which he often quotes, "is sound on the basis of unveiling (*kashf*), but not established by way of transmission (*naql*)" (*Fut.* II. 399, l. 28).

1 Muḥammad b. Qāsim b. ʿAbd al-Raḥmān al-Tamīmī al-Fāsī
He was a well-known Sufi *muḥaddith* in Fez. Ibn ʿArabī met him there on his first visit in 591/1195, and studied al-Tamīmī's book about the saints of the town with him. Al-Tamīmī had spent fifteen years in the East gathering *ḥadīth*, where he had met al-Silafī (see below). He later became imam of the Azhar mosque in Fez. He invested Ibn ʿArabī with the *khirqa* on his second visit to Fez in 593–4/1197–8.[22] He died in 603/1206.
(1, 6, 25, 28, 35, 36, 37)

2 *Abū Ṭāhir Aḥmad b. Muḥammad al-Silafī
He was a very well-known *muḥaddith* of the twelfth century. Born in Isfahan in 478/1085, he studied in Baghdad and then went to live in Alexandria. He became president of a college, which was named after him, and died there in 576/1180. It appears that Ibn ʿArabī may have received *ḥadīth* directly from him, through a written transmission, at the young age of fifteen or sixteen, in the same year that al-Silafī died.[23]
(1, 18, 23, 24, 29, 34, 36, 40)

3 Al-Sharīf Abū Muḥammad Yūnus b. Yaḥyā al-ʿAbbāsī
One of Ibn ʿArabī's closest friends, teachers and companions during his stay in Mecca, he was probably the most influential in the writing of the *Mishkāt al-anwār*. A descendant of the Prophet's family, he was a well-known *muḥaddith* from Baghdad, where he seems to have been a disciple of ʿAbd al-Qādir al-Jīlānī. In addition to *ḥadīth*, he introduced Ibn ʿArabī to the teachings of the Egyptian saint, Dhu'l-Nūn al-Miṣrī. He also invested Ibn ʿArabī with the Qādirite *khirqa* in Mecca in 1202.[24] He died in 608/1211.
(2, 3, 4, 5, 7, 8, 9, 10, 11, 12, 13, 15, 17, 19, 21, 22, 27, 38, 47, 74)

4 Al-Masʿūd ʿAbdallāh Badr al-Ḥabashī
He was one of the closest disciples and a servant of Ibn ʿArabī from their first meeting in Fez in 593/1197 until his death in Malatya (Turkey) in 618/1221. Several works were specifically composed for him, including the *Inshā' al-dawā'ir* and *Ḥilyat al-Abdāl*. He himself wrote one work consisting

22. See the second investiture mentioned in Ibn ʿArabī's *Nasab al-khirqa* (translated by Elmore, *JMIAS*, XXVI).

23. This is according to the information given in Ibn ʿArabī's *al-Kawkab al-durrī fī manāqib Dhi'l-Nūn al-Miṣrī* (translated by R. Deladrière into French as *La Vie Merveilleuse de Dhu'l-Nūn l'Egyptien*, Sindbad 1988, pp. 68 and 385). This implies that Ibn ʿArabī's famous triple vision outside Seville can be dated to this year or before.

24. See the first investiture in the *Nasab al-khirqa*.

of the sayings of Ibn ʿArabī, and was given authority (*riwāya*) to pass on Ibn ʿArabī's writings from the copies he had made.
(3, 10, 21, 25, 33, 35, 37, 39, 40)

5 Muḥammad b. Khālid al-Ṣadafī
This disciple of Ibn ʿArabī originally came from Tlemcen in Algeria. He is mentioned, with al-Ḥabashī, as having requested the writing of the *Ḥilyat al-Abdāl*, which was written in the same year as the *Mishkāt*, 599/1203, during a visit to Ṭā'if, a town some 100 km to the south-east of Mecca.
(5, 8, 9, 12, 15, 19, 22)

6 Abū al-Ḥasan ʿAlī b. ʿAbdallāh b. ʿAbd al-Raḥmān al-Firyābī al-Lakhmī
This *muḥaddith* was one of Ibn ʿArabī's older companions, and is mentioned as present at the Meccan reading of the *Rūḥ al-quds*, dated AH 600. Like Ibn ʿArabī, he was originally from Andalusia and may have been related to the famous Ibn Barrajān. He had also been a student of the Andalusian *muḥaddith*, ʿAbd al-Ḥaqq al-Azdī (see *Fut*. II. 302), copying one of his works in Seville in AH 563. He died in 646/1248.
(7, 13, 20, 26)

7 *Abū Bakr Muḥammad b. ʿAbdallāh b. al-ʿArabī al-Maʿāfirī
He was one of the famous Andalusian *muḥaddithūn* of the twelfth century, but bearing no direct relation to our author. Born in Seville in 468/1076, he travelled with his father to the East, studying in Damascus, Baghdad and Egypt. On his return to Seville, he wrote many books on different subjects, including *ḥadīth*, and became for a time the chief justice (*qāḍī*) of the town. When the Almohads took Seville, he was taken to Marrakesh where he was imprisoned for a year. He died in 543/1148 and was buried in Fez.
(27, 32)

8 Abū Walīd Aḥmad b. al-ʿArabī al-Maʿāfirī
The cousin of the above, he met Ibn ʿArabī in Seville in 1196. He transmitted *ḥadīth* from Abū Bakr Muḥammad b. al-ʿArabī, and gave Ibn ʿArabī authorisation for their transmission.
(14)

9 Al-Zakī b. Abū Bakr al-ʿIrāqī
This person remains unidentified. He may be the same as Yūsuf b. Abū Bakr al-Ḥanafī, who was present at the reading of the *Rūḥ al-quds* in Mecca in AH 600.
(30)

10 ʿAbd al-Wahhāb b. ʿAlī , known as Ibn Sukayna
He was a celebrated Sufi *muḥaddith* from Baghdad. When Ibn ʿArabī first visited the city in AH 601, he made a point of meeting Ibn Sukayna and reading the *Rūḥ al-quds* with him. Since Ibn Sukayna is mentioned here as being one of the transmitters for the *Mishkāt*, written two years before their meeting in Baghdad, we may deduce that the two masters had probably already met in Mecca.[25] He died in 607/1210.
(32, 73)

In addition to the above, the first two introductory *ḥadīth* mention:

11 Abū al-Ḥasan ʿAlī b. Abū al-Fatḥ b. Yaḥyā
A native of Mosul, he appears to have met Ibn ʿArabī in Mecca, since these two *ḥadīth* (which concern the benefit of transmitting forty *ḥadīth*) were the inspiration for the composition of the *Mishkāt*. He is also mentioned as being present at a reading of the *Rūḥ al-quds* in Mosul during Ramadan 601/1205. His father was apparently known as the Canary of Mosul.

It is interesting to note how many of the transmitters (*muḥaddithūn*) who conveyed *ḥadīth* to Ibn ʿArabī had a Sufi or esoteric affiliation. These were men who followed a spiritual path and teaching as well as the discipline of *ḥadīth*. For example, almost all the *ḥadīth* conveyed by Yūnus b. Yaḥyā (no. 3 above) come from one man: Abū al-Waqt ʿAbd al-Awwal b. ʿĪsā al-Sajzī al-Harawī. The latter was born in 458/1066 in Herat. He is reported to have been a pupil of the celebrated Sufi, ʿAbdallāh al-Anṣārī, who wrote the *Manāzil al-Sā'irīn*, but this can only have been indirect because the latter died before he was born. Al-Harawī moved to Baghdad and became a revered transmitter of *ḥadīth* there. When he died in 553/1158, the imam at his funeral was no other than ʿAbd al-Qādir al-Jīlānī.

It is also worth noting the importance of five of the six canonical Sunni collections in Ibn ʿArabī's selection: according to his description, al-Bukhārī, Muslim, al-Tirmidhī, al-Nasā'ī and Abū Dā'ūd account for no less than 45 of the 101 traditions.

25. This deduction is corroborated by the fact that, even though the text of the *Mishkāt* was added to and edited at a later date to incorporate new information, the transmission by Ibn Sukayna was already established in the original Meccan text.

Some of the force of this situation is conveyed by what Ibn ʿArabī writes concerning the last *ḥadīth* in the collection:

> This *ḥadīth* was reported to me several times by the Shaykh, the Imam, scion of the Prophet, transmitter of *ḥadīth*, Abū Muḥammad Yūnus ibn Yaḥyā ... Sometimes I read it aloud to him while he listened, [and this was] in the interior of the Sacred Precinct and facing the most venerated Kaʿba ... He told me that he had received it himself from Abū al-Faḍl Muḥammad ibn ʿUmar.

There then follows the list of transmitters going back to ʿAlī ibn Abī Ṭālib (the companion and son-in-law of the Prophet, and the fourth caliph), who received it from the Prophet. In this way of transmission, a *ḥadīth* is like a light whose flame has been passed from one lamp to another through generations, a living scripture kindled from the "niche-light" of Muhammad.

The passing of this light from generation to generation is a genuine work of prayer and testimony to receptivity. The Prophet Muhammad himself provides the best example of receptivity: as recounted in the thirty-eighth *ḥadīth*, when he received the news of God's saying: "He who greets you with peace, him shall I greet with peace. He who blesses you, him shall I bless", he was in total prostration. His attitude was a model of humility and servanthood before God. The oral transmission of these sayings becomes, then, not just a chain of people passing on information, but more akin to a succession of prostrations. To pass on faithfully what has been given as truth requires a total emptying of self, so that there is no interference on the part of the transmitter. As one scholar has remarked, "the transformative presence of the Prophet, whose emphasis on honesty and integrity was impressed on all who knew him, together with the Quranic warnings against the practice of wilful scriptural distortion which had brought about the destruction of previous religious communities, created an atmosphere of anxious scrupulousness in the reporting of his words and conduct."[26] Many Companions were so afraid of committing mistakes that they refused to relate any *ḥadīth* at all unless it was essential. Others, such as ʿAbdallāh ibn ʿAmr, asked permission from the Prophet himself that they might write down *ḥadīth* to ensure accuracy, even though there was initially discouragement of setting down any scriptural material in writing other than the text of the Qur'an itself.[27] The scrupulous

26. Muhammad Siddiqi, *Ḥadīth Literature*, p. 23.

27. Writing was a rarity in Arabia before Islam, with one report suggesting that only seventeen people knew how to write in Mecca (the most advanced Arab town) in the Prophet's youth. The Prophet himself actively encouraged young people to learn how to read and write (for example, ʿAlī, ʿAbdallāh ibn ʿAmr and Ibn ʿAbbās), and his successors made reading and writing compulsory in the schools that they established.

care taken in the transmission, both oral and written, of *ḥadīth* and *ḥadīth qudsī* springs naturally and directly from revering the light which flowed from and through the Prophet.

For Ibn ʿArabī the reception of a *ḥadīth* did not end with his being able to repeat it correctly word for word. He gave himself unreservedly to the service implied in the words of the Quranic verse: "If you love God, follow me [the Prophet] and then God will love you." In a passage in his *Rūḥ al-quds* Ibn ʿArabī describes his responses to another extraordinary vision which he had in Mecca. It concludes:

> I thanked God for having given me victory over my soul (*nafs*) and said: "O my soul, by the power of Him who gave you a nature inclined to rebellion and made you susceptible to all kinds of blameworthy traits, I swear I shall not leave you in peace until you live up to the teachings of the Book of God and the Way of the Prophet."[28]

God says, in the ninety-first *ḥadīth* reported in this book, "... and when I love him, I become his hearing with which he hears, his sight with which he sees, his hand with which he grasps, and his foot with which he walks." This points to the complete fulfilment of the potential of the human being, and the taste of this is the essence of the gift which this book represents.

28. *Rūḥ al-quds*, p. 23; R. Boase and F. Sahnoun, "Excerpts from the Epistle on the Spirit of Holiness (*Risālah Rūh al-Quds*)", p. 55. For further details, see Hirtenstein, *Unlimited Mercifier*, p. 155.

Bibliography

Translated collections of ḥadīth

Forty Hadith Qudsi. Selected and trans. by Ezzeddin Ibrahim and Denys Johnson-Davies, Cambridge, 1997.

Abū Dā'ūd Sulaymān al-Sijistānī. *Sunan Abū Dā'ūd*, 3 vols. Trans. by Ahmad Hasan, Lahore, 1984.

Al-Bukhārī, Muḥammad. *The Translation of the Meanings of Sahih al-Bukhari*, 9 vols. Trans. by Muhammad Muhsin Khan, Chicago, 1979.

Mālik Ibn Anas. *Al-Muwaṭṭa'*. Trans. by 'Ā'isha 'Abdarrahman at-Tarjumana and Ya'qub Johnson, Norwich, 1982.

Muslim Ibn Ḥajjāj al-Qushayrī. *Ṣaḥīḥ Muslim*. Trans. by 'Abdul Hamid Siddiqi, Lahore, 1971–75.

Al-Nawawī. *Forty Hadith*. Trans. by Ezzeddin Ibrahim and Denys Johnson-Davies. Reprinted Cambridge, 1997.

Other works

Addas, Claude. *Quest for the Red Sulphur: The Life of Ibn 'Arabī*, Cambridge, 1993.

Austin, Ralph W. J. *Sufis of Andalusia*, Partial trans. of Ibn 'Arabī's *Rūḥ al-quds* and *Durrat al-Fākhira*. Reprinted Sherborne, Glos., 1988.

Azami, Muhammad Mustafa. *Studies in Ḥadīth Methodology and Literature*, Indianapolis, 1978.

Beneito, Pablo, and Stephen Hirtenstein. "The Prayer of Blessing [upon the Light of Muhammad] by 'Abd al-'Azīz al-Mahdawī", *JMIAS*, XXXIV, 2003.

Boase, Roger, and Farid Sahnoun. "Excerpts from the Epistle on the Spirit of Holiness (*Risālah Rūh al-Quds*)". In *Muhyiddin Ibn 'Arabi: A Commemorative Volume* (ed. S. Hirtenstein and M. Tiernan), Shaftesbury, Dorset, 1993.

Chittick, William C. *The Self-Disclosure of God: Principles of Ibn al-'Arabī's Cosmology*, Albany, NY, 1998.

—— *The Sufi Path of Knowledge: Ibn al-'Arabī's Metaphysics of Imagination*, Albany, NY, 1989.

Chodkiewicz, M. *An Ocean Without Shore: Ibn 'Arabi, The Book, and the Law*. Trans. from French by David Streight, Albany, NY, 1993.

Denffer, Ahmad Von. *'Ulūm al-Qur'ān*, Leicester, 1994.

Elmore, Gerald T. "*Ḥamd al-ḥamd*: The Paradox of Praise in Ibn al-'Arabī's Doctrine of Oneness". In *Praise* (ed. S. Hirtenstein), Oxford, 1997.

Al-Ghazālī. *Mishkāt al-anwār*. Trans., introduced and annotated by David Buchman as *The Niche of Lights*, with a parallel English–Arabic text, Provo, UT, 1998.

Goldziher, Ignacz. *Muslim Studies*, Vol. 2 (ed. S. M. Stern). Trans. by C. R. Barber and S. M. Stern, Chicago and New York, 1971.

Graham, William A. *Divine Word and Prophetic Word in Early Islam: A Reconsideration of the Sources, with Special Reference to the Divine Saying, or Ḥadīth Qudsī*, The Hague and Paris, 1977.

Guillaume, Alfred. *The Traditions of Islam: An Introduction to the Study of the Hadith Literature*, 1924. Reprinted Salem, NH, 1980.

Hirtenstein, Stephen. *The Unlimited Mercifier: The Spiritual Life and Thought of Ibn 'Arabī*, Oxford, 1999.

Ibn 'Arabī, Muḥyīddīn. *Futūḥāt al-Makkiyya*, Beirut, n.d. Partial critical edition by Osman Yahia, Cairo, 1972–96.

—— *Mishkāt al-anwār*, Arabic text and French trans. by Muhammad Vâlsan as *La Niche des Lumières*, Paris, 1983.

—— *Mishkāt al-anwār*, Cairo, 1999.

—— *Kitāb al-Mubashshirāt*, MS. Zahiriya 5859.

—— *Nasab al-Khirqa*. Trans. by G. Elmore as "Ibn al-'Arabī's Testament on the Mantle of Initiation (*al-Khirqah*)", *JMIAS*, XXVI, 1999.

—— *Rūḥ al-quds*, Damascus, 1986. Partially trans. in R.W. J. Austin, *Sufis of Andalusia*.

—— *Tarjumān al-ashwāq*. Trans. into English, with Arabic text, as *The Tarjumān al-ashwāq: A Collection of Mystical Odes*, by Reynold A. Nicholson, London, 1911. Reprinted 1978.

Morris, James Winston. "Seeking God's Face", Parts I and II, *JMIAS*, XVI, 1994, and XVII, 1995.

Siddiqi, Muhammad Z. *Ḥadīth Literature: Its Origin, Development, Special Features and Criticism*, Calcutta, 1961.

Wensinck, A. J. *A Handbook of Early Muhammadan Tradition*, Leiden, 1960.

Yahia, Osman. *Histoire et Classification de l'Oeuvre d'Ibn 'Arabī*, Damascus, 1964.

Yilmaz, Hasan Kamil. *Tasavvufi Hadîs Şerhleri ve Konevînin Kirk Hadîs Şerhi*, Istanbul, 1990.

Index of first lines

The *Mishkāt* numbers are in bold

I shall not bring two fears together upon a servant (**11**)
I shall not make him go forth to fight except for My sake (**81**)
If I deprive My servant of his two eyes in this lower world (**34**)
If My servant has lost his state of purity and does not make an ablution (**64**)
If My servant intends a good deed, then I count it for him as a good deed (**57**)
If you possessed everything on earth, would you then redeem yourself (**14**)
Look at the prayer of My servant and see if he has completed it or if he has omitted anything (**72**)
Moses, upon him be peace, said, "O Lord, teach me something by which I can invoke You and pray to You." (**85**)
My love is by necessity for those who love one another in Me (**88**)
My Mercy and Compassion prevail over My Anger (**47**)
My servant has hastened to Me by his own doing (**45**)
My true servant is the one who is in remembrance of Me (**46**)
[O Abraham] what is this terrible fear you have? (**41**)
O child of Adam, as long as you beseech Me and hope for Me, I shall forgive you whatever you have done (**28**)
O child of Adam, devote yourself exclusively to My worship (**39**)
O child of Adam, do not fear for lack of nourishment, for My treasuries are full (**65**)
O child of Adam, each one wants you for himself, and I want you for yourself (**50**)
O child of Adam, have no fear of one who holds power, when My Power endures permanently (**67**)
O child of Adam, have you ever seen any good? (**51**)
O child of Adam, how can you deem Me weak? (**63**)
O child of Adam, I created you of dust, then of sperm, and your creation cost Me no effort (**52**)
O child of Adam, I have created you for My sake, and I have created things for your sake (**58**)
O child of Adam, I strike you with three blows (**73**)
O child of Adam, I was sick, and you did not visit Me (**98**)
O child of Adam, if you are content with what I have apportioned you (**48**)
O child of Adam, if you give generously of the surplus you have (**64**)
O child of Adam, if only you were to see how little is left of your appointed time (**47b**; see n. 2, p. 84)
O child of Adam, it is your right from Me that I be a lover for you (**54**)
O child of Adam, just as I do not make demands on you regarding what you will do tomorrow, so do not make demands on Me (**59**)
O child of Adam, perform four prostrations in your prayer (**62**)
O child of Adam, when you remember Me you are grateful to Me (**8**)
O child of Adam, you owe Me obligations, and I owe you nourishment (**61**)
O child of Adam, you shall not be safe from My ruse until you have traversed the Path (**68**)
O David, caution the children of Israel against eating out of desire (**42**)
O Israfil, by My Might and Majesty, by My Generosity and Liberality, for one who recites 'In the name of God, the All-Compassionate, the Most Merciful' (**6**)
[O Moses] I shall teach you five sayings which constitute the pillars of Religion (**74**)
O My servants, I have forbidden injustice to Myself (**1**)

Where are those who have loved each other for the sake of My Majesty? (**12**)
Whoever demeans one of My Saints has declared war on Me (**76**)
Whoever says: "There is no god but God" and "God is greater", his Lord confirms his truthfulness (**40**)
Whoever treats a friend of Mine as an enemy, on him I declare war (**91**)
You are the faithful who rest in security, and I am God the Faithful who bestows security (**55**)
You are the guardians of My servant's deeds, but I am the Watcher (**96**)
You may be either prophet–servant or prophet–king (**75**)